Jack David and

Jack David is the president of ECW Press and teaches English at Centennial College in Toronto. He has written essays on bpNichol, Earle Birney, John Barth, and visual poetry. Robert Lecker teaches English at McGill University in Montreal. His book, *On the Line: Readings in the Short Fiction of Clark Blaise, John Metcalf, and Hugh Hood,* was published in 1982.

Together, David and Lecker edit the critical journal *Essays on Canadian Writing* as well as *The Annotated Bibliography of Canada's Major Authors* and (with Ellen Quigley) *Canadian Writers and Their Works.*

Alex Colville

Alex Colville was born in Toronto in 1920, but moved to the Maritimes with his parents when he was a child. He received a degree in Fine Arts from Mount Allison University in Sackville, New Brunswick. After serving in the army during World War II, he returned to Mount Allison, where he taught for seventeen years. An outstanding modern artist, he is as well known abroad as he is in Canada.

New Press Canadian Classics

Distinguished by the use of Canadian fine art on its covers, New Press Canadian Classics is an innovative, much-needed series of high-quality, reasonably priced editions of the very best Canadian fiction, nonfiction, and poetry.

New Press Canadian Classics

Hubert Aquin *The Antiphonary,* Alan Brown (trans.)

Margaret Atwood *Surfacing*

Sandra Birdsell *Night Travellers*

Constance Beresford-Howe *The Marriage Bed*

Marie-Claire Blais *Nights in the Underground,* Ray Ellenwood (trans.)

Clark Blaise *A North American Education, Tribal Justice*

Matt Cohen *The Expatriate*

George Elliott *The Kissing Man*

Mavis Gallant *My Heart Is Broken*

Anne Hébert *Héloise,* Sheila Fischman (trans.), *In the Shadow of the Wind,* Sheila Fischman (trans.) *Kamouraska,* Norman Shapiro (trans.)

David Helwig *The Glass Knight, Jennifer, It Is Always Summer*

Hugh Hood *White Figure, White Ground, You Can't Get There from Here, A New Athens, Reservoir Ravine, Black and White Keys*

M.T. Kelly *I Do Remember the Fall*

Martin Kevan *Racing Tides*

Robert Kroetsch *Alibi, Badlands*

Félix Leclerc *The Madman, the Kite & the Island,* Philip Stratford (trans.)

Hugh MacLennan *Voices in Time, Each Man's Son, The Watch That Ends the Night, Two Solitudes*

Keith Maillard *Alex Driving South, Cutting Through, The Knife in My Hands*

Antonine Maillet *Pélagie,* Philip Stratford (trans.)

Gwendolyn MacEwen *Noman*

Brian Moore *An Answer from Limbo*

Ken Norris (Ed.) *Canadian Poetry Now*

Leon Rooke *Fat Woman, Shakespeare's Dog*

Reorge Ryga *The Ecstasy of Rita Joe and Other Plays*

Carol Shields *Various Miracles*

Audrey Thomas *Intertidal Life*

Helen Weinzweig *Basic Black with Pearls*

new press CANADIAN CLASSICS

Canadian Poetry
Volume Two

Edited by Jack David and Robert Lecker
Introduction by George Woodcock

Published in 1994 by
Stoddart Publishing Co. Limited
34 Lesmill Road
Toronto, Canada
M3B 2T6
(416) 445-3333

Canadian Cataloguing in Publication Data

Main entry under title:

Canadian poetry

(New Press Canadian classics)
ISBN 0-7736-7417-9 (v. 1)   ISBN 0-7736-7418-7 (v. 2)

1. Canadian poetry (English) — 20th century.*
2. Canadian poetry (English) — 19th century.*
I. David, Jack, 1946-   .   II. Lecker, Robert,
1951-   .   III. Series.

PS8273.C35 1994   C811'.508   C94-930408-5
PR9195.25.C35 1994

General Paperbacks/ECW Press
edition published in 1982
Reprinted in February 1989

Printed and bound in the United States of America

*Stoddart Publishing gratefully acknowledges the
support of the Canada Council, Ontario Ministry of
Culture, Tourism, and Recreation, Ontario Arts Council,
and Ontario Publishing Centre in the development of
writing and publishing in Canada.*

Contents

JAMES REANEY b. 1926

ROBERT KROETSCH b. 1927

PHYLLIS WEBB b. 1927

D. G. JONES b. 1929

JAY MACPHERSON b. 1931

ALDEN NOWLAN b. 1933

JOE ROSENBLATT b. 1933

LEONARD COHEN b. 1934

GEORGE BOWERING b. 1935

JOHN NEWLOVE b. 1938

MARGARET ATWOOD b. 1939

bill bissett b. 1939

PATRICK LANE b. 1939

DENNIS LEE b. 1939

GWENDOLYN MACEWEN b. 1941

DAPHNE MARLATT b. 1942

MICHAEL ONDAATJE b. 1943

bpNICHOL b. 1944

Canadian Poetry

An Introduction to Volume Two

[handwritten: 1930 - 1980]

Perhaps the most striking characteristic of Canadian poetry over the past five or six decades had been its extraordinary continuity. The first quarter of the twentieth century was a barren time, in which no new poets of any marked power or originality emerged. But with the almost simultaneous appearance in 1923 of E. J. Pratt's first book, *Newfoundland Verse* and of the *McGill Fortnightly Review*—under the editorship of A. J. M. Smith and F. R. Scott—as a vehicle for the modernist verse that was just beginning to emerge in Canada, a flow of new and vital poetry began that has broadened and deepened as the decades have gone on.

[handwritten margin notes: clear line of Dev. of white; Modernist line of Dev.]

The poets represented in Volume Two of *Canadian Poetry* belong mainly to the latter part of this period, and most of them made their names in the late 1950s or afterwards. But there are enough exceptions to illustrate the continuity of which I have been speaking. Two of the poets in Volume Two—Louis Dudek and Raymond Souster—belonged during the later 1940s to the same *First Statement* group in Montreal as Irving Layton (Volume One). Margaret Avison (Volume One) published her first book and became known as a poet years after such considerably younger writers as James Reaney and Jay Macpherson (Volume Two). As I already remarked in my Introduction to Volume One, there are writers like Earle Birney and Dorothy Livesay and P. K. Page who first began to publish in the 1930s and 1940s but are perhaps best known for works done in their brilliant second careers in the 1960s and 1970s. And there are other writers, like Irving Layton, whose creative life presents an unbroken continuity from the 1940s down to the present.

Yet the period from the mid-1950s onward, which embraces the careers of most of the poets appearing in the second volume of *Canadian Poetry*, differs from the immediately preceding decades in a number of striking ways. To begin with, there has been the remarkable increase in the amount of

poetry written and published and in the number of activ
poets. Early modernist poetry in Canada, like the modernis
movement everywhere, tended to be self-consciously anti
popular, and this meant that poets during this period did no
retain the kind of followings that had made best-sellers out o
earlier verse-writers of such varied talents as Charles G. D
Roberts, Bliss Carman, and Pauline Johnson. Moreover, th
development of the movement more or less coincided with th
onset of the depression, which adversely affected Canadia
publishing and made the industry less inclined than ever t
bring out experimental or minority-oriented writing of an
kind. This meant that even such important poets of the 1930
as A. J. M. Smith and F. R. Scott could not publish collection
of their work during that decade; Smith's first book of verse
News of the Phoenix, did not appear until 1943, and Scott'
Overture not until 1950. It was this situation that led the poet
of the time to put their own money into magazines lik
Preview and *First Statement* and into small presses like th
Contact Press which Layton, Dudek, and Souster founded i
1952 for the publication of contemporary poetry.

Such poet-directed efforts preluded the extraordinary out
burst of poetry writing and publishing that began late in th
1950s and proliferated extraordinarily during the 1960s an
1970s. Some figures which I included in my essay or
"Poetry" in the second edition of *Literary History of Canad*
give an idea of the rapidly changing situation. I began with
considering 1959, the year in which I founded *Canadiar
Literature*.

In 1959, 24 books of English verse were published in
Canada; most of them appeared with the established
houses. Round about 1963 the growth in publication was
sharply evident, and in 1970 more than 120 books of
verse were published, a five-fold increase in a decade.
Only a small proportion of these books now came from
the trade publishers.

In my research I found that during the period between 196(
and 1973 alone no less than 590 poets had published ove

1,100 books of verse, not counting anthologies, and I hazarded what I think was probably the conservative guess that if one counted poets whose work had appeared in magazines but not yet in one-writer collections, the number of poets writing *and* publishing in that period would be nearer to 1,000, which, as I remarked,

> carries us a long way from the situation as late as the early 1960s when, as Louis Dudek said, 'Twenty or so poets might be thought to represent all the reputable poetry of the country.'

This outburst of poetic creation was assisted by a change in the infrastructure of the Canadian literary world, by the emergence of many more poet-edited magazines and poet-directed presses, which were largely encouraged and sustained by the opportune appearance of the Canada Council in 1957. I am not suggesting that the Canada Council was in any direct way responsible for the poetic upsurge; patron-artist relationships are never as simple as that, while in periods of great artistic activity the patrons seem to be as much influenced by the *zeitgeist* as the artists themselves. And there is no doubt that the later 1960s and the 1970s were a time when the public status of poetry did change considerably. As I further remarked in *Literary History of Canada*:

> Nowadays poetry is not merely—in number of titles—the most published of all genres in Canada; it sells more reliably than fiction, and poets, recently derided, have become something very near to culture heroes, especially among the young, so that almost any modestly-known verse-writer can attract to a reading of his work enough poetry fanciers to fill reasonably large lecture halls on most Canadian campuses and in most Canadian towns sophisticated enough to possess art galleries.

Poetry at that time tended to be associated with the currently fashionable movements in society. There were clear links—notably in a common preoccupation with "happen-ings"—between the new poetry of the time and the counter-culture that began with the flower children. But in fact the poets were following their own courses, and only one of the poets repesented in *Canadian Poetry*, bill bissett, has consist-ently followed the role of a counter-cultural leader. Simil-arly, for a time at least, a number of the poets, here collect-ed—notably Margaret Atwood, Dennis Lee, and Milton Acorn—showed sympathies with the Canadian nationalism that flourished especially during the 1960s and 1970s, but in hind-sight it is not the political overtones of their work that seem important.

In some ways the situation has changed in the 1980s. Recession economics have made verse a little more difficult to publish, and the popularity of poetry seems to have receded somewhat if one can judge by sales of books and the size of audiences at poetry readings. But the situation has not re-turned, and is unlikely to return, where a poet of proved ability like Scott or Smith would have to wait more than a decade for the first appearance of his book. Moreover, poetry in Canada has received in recent years a degree of critical and academic attention that would have been hard to imagine in 1959, the year when I founded *Canadian Literature* and was widely told that the journal would fail for lack of poets and novelists to write about. The result of all these changes is that in 1982 poetry as a genre enjoys an unprecedented standing within the general world of Canadian writing, and an unpre-cedented international repute.

All this could not have happened if the great expansion of poetry had been merely a matter of numbers. As Northrop Frye remarked, "Such a quantitative increase eventually makes for a qualitative change ..." and while one clearly cannot say that Canadian poetry is better because there are more poets, one can say two other things with fair confidence in the facts bearing one out. One is that in any period of wide artistic productivity the kind of mental excitement that pre-vails tends to stimulate poets to write at the height of their ability, so that even if the bad poets do not become good, the good poets may become better. The other is that, while the majority of the 1,000 poets I mentioned earlier as emerging between 1960 and 1973 were perhaps not exceptional, the proportion of excellent writing in relation to the expanding whole did not seem to diminish, so that now we actually do have in quantitative terms many more good poets than we were aware of two decades ago. The contents of this volume, which includes only a selection of our best recent poets, is a demonstration of this fact.

It is appropriate that Volume Two of *Canadian Poetry* should begin with Louis Dudek and Raymond Souster among the first three names in its contents list, for their presence emphasizes that the connection between a revival of Canadian poetry and the involvement of Canadians even peripherally in the movement we call nationalism was not accidental. A genuinely Canadian poetry could not have evolved if the poets had remained oriented to the traditional goals of colonial writers. Liberation in the sense of finding a voice appropriate to the realities of Canadian experience demanded an experimental approach, and the lead for such an approach had to be found in the modernist and quasi-modernist movements outside Canada.

The earlier Canadian modernists had tended to look toward British models. One observed the influence of Eliot and Yeats and Auden not only in Smith and Scott, but in Dorothy Livesay and P. K. Page as well, and it was no accident that one of the most important early poetry magazines, *Preview*, should have been dominated by the English poet, transient in Canada, Patrick Anderson. The rival *First Statement* group rejected British influences, preferring to find its lead among New World poets, and this was the beginning of Ezra Pound's intermittent role as a model for Canadian poets; it was to be revived in the 1960s, filtered through Black Mountain glass, among the group around the magazine *Tish* in Vancouver, represented in *Canadian Poetry* by George Bowering. Neither Dudek nor Souster, at least in his mature poetry, appears as a mere imitator of Pound; indeed, the difference between their styles shows how each has taken one aspect of Pound and transformed it for his own poetic purposes. Louis Dudek is more the philosophic poet, concerned with historic issues on a global scale, and so it is the Pound of the *Cantos* whose distant echo we sometimes catch, though what is actually said is an evident projection of Dudek's highly individual sensibility.

I seem to peer through time, as through a tottering mansion,
to glimpse the shapes beyond, the spectral bone-men
       who lived, and died, and believed.

And see the new religion fearfully replacing the old,
       burning temples,
knowing, past cure, how sure their reasons were
       against the old idols,
 who are now burned themselves, with the sure fire of reason.

Nothing stands, we say, we moderns.
All's flux, an art of mathematics — of fiery matter,
while the old gods gutter and die in the flames.

It is an earlier Pound — Pound the Imagist — who stands in the shadows behind Raymond Souster's poetry. Souster had refined and adapted imagism, turning it into a remarkable instrument for bringing the visible world clearly alive in our minds while giving it a transparency through which we see the poet's mind ironically reflecting, with the thought always a consequence of the experience. Souster had written so eloquently of Toronto and its life that he has really become that rare phenomenon, an urban regional poet, charting the city's moods and mirages in poems like "Downtown Corner Newsstand," yet always remaining that indrawn person whose private dreams emerge in pieces such as "Where the Blue Horses."

So for now
nothing but sleep and dreams and thoughts of sleep,
not even love keeps us awake tonight,

as we sink into that strange land
where the blue horses toss
riderless and proud.

Al Purdy is an example of the way a good poet can be stimulated and changed by a mood of excitement and innovation such as existed during the 1960s. Purdy's early verse was conventional and constrained, but during the late 1950s, when he was already forty, his style began to develop rapidly. He was eclectic in his acceptance of influences, and perhaps the greatest influence of all was that of the audiences on whom, on reading circuits, he tried out his verse. He developed a manner as individual as any in Canadian poetry. Purdy writes very directly from experience, so that his poems often read like fragments of autobiography or travelogue, and he adds to a fluently colloquial manner a range of moods that can shift with fascinating rapidity from the melancholic to the comic, from the romantic to the deadpan realist.

Purdy had been a great influence on younger poets, largely because of his ability to meld the sense of history, of which Canadians have become knowingly conscious in recent decades, with the awareness of place as a visual reality; there is a haunting love of the land in his poems that is more telling than any stridently nationalist verse can be.

Old fences drift vaguely among the trees
   a pile of moss-covered stones
gathered for some ghost purpose
has lost meaning under the meaningless sky
   —they are like cities under water
and the undulating green waves of time
   are laid on them

At one time, in the early 1960s, there was much talk about a mythopoeic school of poets greatly influenced by the critical theories of Northrop Frye. The poets most often named in this connection were James Reaney, Jay Macpherson, and Eli Mandel. Frye has repudiated the role of guru in this connection and rightly pointed out that the opinions of critics never lead to poetry. And, while it is true that all these poets have made a considerable use of mythology and have even invented myths to serve their purposes, they are certainly not wholly mythological in their preoccupations, and in their actual achievements hardly more so than a poet like Al Purdy who, for all his resolute down-to-earthness, has created some notable myths in poetic form about Loyalist Canada and its heirs.

In fact, now that the talk about myth has died down, it is not easy to consider Reaney, Macpherson, and Mandel as in any way forming or having formed a movement. Reaney, seen in perspective, with his plays given equal weight to his lyric poetry, seems essentially a parodist of the bucolic mode, whimsical and capricious in his use of memories of country life and fantasies about it. A preoccupation with myth as opposed to historic actuality does hang over everything he writes, but within that framework the variations are considerable, from the Gothic fantasy of "Antichrist as a Child" to the metaphysical symbolism of "The Red Heart," and the oddly naive mockery of "The Royal Visit."

There is an air of cultivated innocence about Reaney's poetry that can often be disturbing. Macpherson and Mandel do not share this characteristic. The influence of Blake is strong on Jay Macpherson, but it is the Blake of powerful visions to whom she has been listening without any surrender of intellectual acuity, so that her poems are memorable for their wit and conceit and even for their irreverant handling of the myths.

> Goddess of crossways, three-faced, was it you my
> Muse all this while? you are the last who hallows
> Contents of pockets, broken dolls, dead puppies,
>   Queen, garbage-eater. ("Hecate Trivia.")

Perhaps Eli Mandel has been the most literally mythological of the three, in the narrow sense that his poems are often invented tales meant to convey some meaning too deep for statement, as in "Marina" and "Notes from the Underground." But often they are most effective, in a bitterly astringent way, when they take some real incident, or some memory, as in "estevan, 1934," and reach into it for the hidden kernel, which in this case is the essential difference between the ordinary settlers and the métis woman who spoke little and touched often

even when the sun killed
cattle and rabbis
                    even
in poisoned slow air
like hunters
            like lizards
they touched   stone
they touched
                earth

Some of the poets of this period are remarkable for their power of abstracting from existence a tight and detached artifact of words, dense with feeling. In the poems of D. G. Jones one is always conscious of a highly lapidary quality, of every word being economically counted and used to the full extent of its potency, of every image deliberately meagre, so that one can say of him, as he does of another poet in "Portrait of Anne Hébert,"

Your sensibility
has the sure fingers of the blind:

Each decision
Cuts like a scalpel
Through tangled emotion.

Phyllis Webb, a poet up to now greatly under-rated, has offered a small but exquisite production of poems high in moral intensity and intense even in doubt, as in that mordant meditation, "The Shape of Prayer."

The shape of prayer
is like the shape of the small
beach stone, rounded smooth, but individual
in its despair,
skimmed on the water it skips to drown
down with its sunken fellows, down
in despair.

The shape of prayer is that—
curved and going nowhere, to fall
in pure abstraction saying everything
and saying nothing at all.

A striking feature of the 1960s and 1970s is the number of
important poets who have come from outside the middle class
and the academic community. Milton Acorn, Alden Nowlan,
and Patrick Lane, as well as Al Purdy, attended no university
and have a direct knowledge of the life of poverty and manual
work. It is rash to generalize from such shared backgrounds.
The experience of poverty ("I've tasted my blood too
much / to love what I was born to") led Milton Acorn into
Marxist-Leninist politics; it led Patrick Lane to write a poem
entitled "I Am Tired of Your Politics" in which he said:

Shall we sing other than
our lives? Peace, wisdom,
excellence in the small
affairs of the heart?

Not to "sing other than our lives" seems almost a rule with
such poets. It leads them to a regionalism, almost a localism,
of approach, out of which have emerged the extraordinary
poems by Purdy on the Ontarian hinterland, by Nowlan on
the Maritimes, by Lane on the land between the Rockies and
the Pacific. In Lane it produced a stoic pessimism that has not
ruled out the most intense compassion for the dispossessed,
whether men or women rejected by society or animals living
under the harsh laws of nature or the threat of man's preda-
tion. Lane's "Wild Horses" and Nowlan's "The Bull Moose"
speak alike the extraordinary empathy for the wilderness that
has permeated so much of recent Canadian poetry. Nowlan's
bull moose, recognizing his own death, comes out of the wilds
into the village, where the people pet and persecute him until

... just as the sun dropped in the river
the bull moose gathered his strength
like a scaffolded king, straightened and lifted his horns

so that even the wardens backed away as they raised their
   rifles.
When he roared, people ran to their cars. All the young
   men
leaned on their automobile horns as he toppled.

In others of these poets the sense of locality is strong. Robert Kroetsch is as experimental in his verse as in his novels, but in each he remains close to his prairie background, and the sense of vast spaces and of an equally vast if unrecorded background permeates many of his works, such as "Stone Hammer Poem," in which the poet discusses an Indian stone maul on his desk, dug up by his father.

It is a stone
old as the last
Ice Age, the
retreating/ the
retreating ice,
the retreating
buffalo, the
retreating Indians

For the poet all that happened to the land, all that happened to his father, even to himself, are embodied in that hammer.

Sometimes I use it
in the (hot) wind
(to hold down paper)

smelling a little of cut
grass or maybe even of
ripening wheat or of
buffalo blood hot
in the dying sun.

Sometimes I write
my poems for that

stone hammer.

The emphasis in the kind of poetry I have been discussing lies largely in the content. The poet seeks to present symbolically a view of the world, an idea of life; clear and careful craftsmanship, the limpid voice, verse like a windowpane (to adapt Orwell) are important; we have to see through the curtain of words. Such verse tends to be innovatory only in so far as it clears away the artificialities of traditional poetics. Indeed, a too experimental approach, that dislocates the conversational or descriptive modes, can frustrate the purpose of such poets. Even a poet given greatly to experiment, like Earle Birney, tends to avoid it in the poems where he is setting out to tell a significant incident or to make a statement about life. Most literary experimentation, of course, is directed towards making statements about art.

And so we come to another kind of poetry represented in this volume—the innovatory work of writers like bpNichol and Joe Rosenblatt and, to a less extent, Michael Ondaatje, George Bowering, and Daphne Marlatt. For Nichol the content of the poem is essentially what others would regard as its form—the way it looks and sounds. Myth, symbol, and image become as irrelevant as message or moral. Ultimately, even, the form of the poem loses its necessity. As Nichol says in a rare didactic moment:

the poem begins & ends nowhere
being part of the flow you live with

Nevertheless, there are distinct shapes to Nichol's poems, sometimes on the page and sometimes in the ear, and with his work we are clearly moving into a contested borderland between concrete poetry, conceptual art, and modern music. Joe Rosenblatt differs notably from Nichol in his use of visual images and his comic juxtaposition of them; he is perhaps the nearest Canada has to a true surrealist poet. Michael Ondaatje takes some of the surrealist insights, but builds them into structures of narrative or of ironic reflection, so that the absurd representation of actuality becomes a vehicle of poetic insight, of imaginative liberation, as Ondaatje himself saw in the paintings of Henri Rousseau le Douanier.

They are the ideals of dreams.
Among the exactness,
the symmetrical petals,
the efficiently flying angels,
there is a complete liberation.
The parrot is interchangeable;
tomorrow in its place
a waltzing man and tiger,
brash legs of a bird.

George Bowering and Daphne Marlatt were both closely involved in the *Tish* movement in the Vancouver 1960s, which was much influenced by Charles Olson's theories of poetry as a structure of syllable and breath. The principal effect on Bowering was to produce a tense lyrical form, with the theory unobtrusive:

I think of
Troilus & Cressida
cursing the sun —
rise from their hurricaned bed;
he to clatter away
on his army horse,
she to pick
her sunny way home —

Daphne Marlatt's poems vary between extremely terse, short-lined notations, a kind of shorthand of the emotions, and attempts to project a collective consciousness in her prose-form poem about the life of a fishing settlement, "Steveston," one of the most interesting of Canadian long poems.

The poets I have so far left unmentioned hardly form a group, since their achievements have been highly individual, and they have tended, in what is perhaps a characteristically Canadian manner, to mingle the traditional and the innovatory, using pragmatically the approach that in any poem best served their intent.

Leonard Cohen and Gwendolyn MacEwen have in common, for instance, that they began to write, to publish and to be recognized early, so that they have been figures in the poetic world for the past two decades. They are both romantics in temperament, but from that point their approaches diverge.

Cohen's preoccupation with the lyrical element in poetry led him out of books into song writing and a popular performer's career. As a result his romanticism often tipped over into sentimentality, but at the same time the rich denseness of his early poetry (in *Let Us Compare Mythologies*) was sweated away, and the poems by him most likely to survive are perhaps less the love lyrics which now seem facile than the bleak poems of anger against a world order he has come to hate.

> You have your drugs
> You have your guns
> You have your Pyramids and your Pentagons
> With all your grass and bullets
> you cannot hunt us any more
> All that we disclose of ourselves forever
> is this warning
> Nothing that you built has stood
> Any system you can contrive without us
> will be brought down

Critics have observed the extraordinary surface brilliance of the poems of Gwendolyn MacEwen. It is not merely the accomplishment of practice; it is a natural ability to build harmonious structures of words that create agreeable emotional responses, and so lead one into the strange country of the mind which she perpetually creates and recreates. As she warns herself as well as her reader:

precede me into this elusive country,
travel the tracks of my old laughter,
tame this landscape, and I will follow after—
yet do not let this desert inherit you,
absorb your caravan into sand—
(which is your body, which is the land?)

The elusive country MacEwen mostly travels is the borderland between now and then, between the present and the ancient cultures that have always fascinated her and filled her poetry not only with mythologies and symbols but also with the sense of a compelling intermediary world of magic and dream, a world out of which her exotic novels and short stories have been drawn.

A different kind of romanticism inspires John Newlove. There is something in him of the late nineteenth-century decadents as he writes of joyless pleasures, but without the hard pessimistic edge of Patrick Lane. Yet he was one of the first poets to follow T. E. Hulme's injunction and bring out the poetry latent in the vast spaces and long roads of the Canadian West—to enter into the nature of the land, to see the moral character of its history, the guilts and failures of those who inhabit it, the restlessness that the vast dimensions breed—

    never
to be at ease, but always migrating
from city to city
seeking some almost seen
god or food or earth or word.

In the early days of Canadian poetry Bliss Carman celebrated the happy vagabond; it is a sign of the disillusionment accompanying the maturing of a tradition that Newlove celebrates the melancholy wanderer.

There is a more clear-edged rejection of our society in Dennis Lee's poems, and one can regard him as the only really successful Canadian political poet, perhaps because he has never written as a partisan, but has seen the ills of society in moral and social terms. Often he has quite deliberately, as in "1838," used with effect the conventional form of the political ballad, but he has also developed the long free argumentative line employed so effectively in *Civil Elegies*. Lee's anger at what men have made of life is related to his enjoyment of living, which emerges in his children's verses (not represented here) and in a poem like "Summer Song," which declares how the beauty of life negates none of its sorrows yet is there for our joy.

> Breath and death and pestilence
> Were not revoked by that.
> Heavy things went on, among
> The calm magnificat.
> Yet as I sat, my body spoke
> The words of my return:
> *There is a joy of being, which you*
> *Must be still and learn.*

Margaret Atwood's role has been confused by the fame she has acquired in other fields, as a novelist, as an innovatory critic of Canadian writing, as a public personality. Her reputation in other fields of writing is not undeserved, but it has tended to obscure the excellence of her verse, read by a much smaller and largely a different audience from her fiction. Over the years since *The Circle Game* won the Governor-General's Award in 1966, her poetry has sustained an extraordinary level of sparse discipline. It is unobtrusively experimental in the manner of a poet seeking always the appropriate form for the myth or the thought she is concerned with. This fastidious formalism is combined with a certain didacticism; the tough and resilient phrasing combines with psychological realism and a considerable visual sensibility to present a clear-sighted view of human relations, astringent yet compassionate. Atwood's poems are pervaded by a sense of mythic and historic unity with mankind, often unknown yet understood through feeling.

This forest is alien
to me, closer than skin,
unknown, something early
as caves and buried, hard,

a chipped stone knife, the
long bone lying in darkness
inside my right arm: not
innocent but latent.

The laconic tone, the sufficiency of statement, the truth
so slightly and yet so powerfully stated, mark Atwood as
one of Canada's best poets and one of the best poets writing
anywhere in English today.

George Woodcock

Acknowledgments

*We wish to thank the following authors, publishers, and copyright holders
for permission to reproduce the poems in this book.*

LOUIS DUDEK: "The Pomegranate," selections from *Europe* — 19, 95,
"Coming Suddenly to the Sea" from *Collected Poems*, selections from
Atlantis — 42, 45, 96 from *Poems from Atlantis*, and "The Jungle," "Life &
Art," "Autumn," from *Cross-Section*; all poems by permission of the
author. AL PURDY: "The Cariboo Horses," "The Country North of
Belleville," "Song of the Impermanent Husband," "Necropsy of Love"
from *The Cariboo Horses*, "Wilderness Gothic," "Elegy for a Grandfather,"
"Lament for the Dorsets" from *Wild Grape Wine*, "Trees at the Arctic
Circle," "Eskimo Graveyard" from *North of Summer*, "Inside the Mill"
from *Sundance at Dusk*, and "The Road to Newfoundland" from *Being
Alive*, all poems reprinted by permission of The Canadian Publishers,
McClelland and Stewart Limited, Toronto. RAYMOND SOUSTER: "Where
the Blue Horses," "Yonge Street Saturday Night," "Downtown Corner
Newsstand," "Two Dead Robins," "Study: The Bath," "Armadale Avenue
Revisited," "Pigeons on George Street" are reprinted from the *Collected
Poems of Raymond Souster* by permission of Oberon Press. ELI MANDEL:
"Earthworms Eat Earthworms and Learn," "Agatha Christie," "estevan,
1934:" from *Stony Plain*, "birthmark:," "the double world:" from *Out of
Place*, and " 'Grandfather's Painting': David Thauberger," "Parting at
Udaipur: the Lake Palace," "In My 57th Year" from *Life Sentence*, all ©
Press Porcépic by permission of the publisher; "Notes from the Under-
ground," "Marina" from *Dreaming Backwards*, © General Publishing by

Description" by permission of General Publishing; "Did" reprinted by permission of The Canadian Publishers, McClelland and Stewart Limited, Toronto. JOHN NEWLOVE: "The Prairie," "Crazy Riel," "Harry, 1967," "The Cave," "The Flowers," "Samuel Hearne in Wintertime," from *The Fat Man*, and "Notes From and Among the Wars," "That There Is No Relaxation" from *Lies*, all poems by permission of the author.
MARGARET ATWOOD: "A Night in the Royal Ontario Museum," "Progressive Insanities of a Pioneer," "The Animals in That Country" from *The Animals in That Country*; "After Jaynes" from *Two-Headed Poems*; "Trainride, Vienna-Bonn" from *True Stories*; and "There Is Only One of Everything" from *You are Happy* © Oxford University Press, Canada, by permission of the publisher; "A Sibyl," "This Is a Photograph of Me," "Some Objects of Wood and Stone" © Margaret Atwood, 1966 (Toronto: House of Anansi). bill bissett: "Tell me what attackd yu," The Canadian," [untitled concrete visual], "Killer Whale," "a pome in praise of all quebec bombers," "th tomato conspiracy aint worth a whol pome," from *Beyond Even Faithful Legends: Selected Poems*; "whos out tonite;" from *northern birds in color*; and "Evolution of Letters Chart" from *pass th food release th spirit book*, all poems by permission of the author. PATRICK LANE: "Elephants," "Wild Horses," from *Separations*, "I Am Tired of Your Politics" from *The Measure*; "Loving She Stood Apart" from *Letters from the Savage Mind*; "Mountain Oysters" from *Mountain Oysters*; "At the Edge of the Jungle" from *Unborn Things*; and "Thirty Below" from *Poems New and Selected*, all poems by permission of the author. DENNIS LEE: selections from *Civil Elegies* "2, 9," from *Civil Elegies* (Toronto: House of Anansi, 1972); "400: Coming Home," "1838" "Thursday," "The Gods," "Remember, Woman," "Summer Song," from *The Gods*, reprinted by permission of The Canadian Publishers, McClelland and Stewart Limited, Toronto. GWENDOLYN MacEWEN: "Tall Tales" from *T. E. Lawrence Poems* by permission of Mosaic Press; "Eden, Eden," "Poems in Braille," "The Caravan," "The Shadow-Maker," "The Armies of the Moon," "As the Angels," from *Magic Animals* by permission of Gage Publishing. DAPHNE MARLATT: "Constellation" from *What Matters: Writing 1969-70*, Coach House Press, 1980, by permission of the author; "for k, d," "so cocksure," "sculptural energy is the mountain," "At Birch Bay," "New Moon," "seeing your world from the outside," "light writes," from *Net Work* by permission of Talon Books. MICHAEL ONDAATJE: "The Diverse Causes," "Henri Rousseau and Friends," "In Another Fashion," "Peter," "'The Gate in His Head,'" "King Kong Meets Wallace Stevens," "Spider Blues," "White Dwarfs," "Letters & Other Worlds," © Michael Ondaatje from *There's a Trick with a Knife I'm Learning to Do* (McClelland and Stewart, 1979). bpNICHOL: "1335 Comox Avenue," "Dada Lama," "Blues," "Two Words: A Wedding" from *Selected Poems*; "late night summer poem" from *The Other Side of the Room*; "A Small Song That Is His" from *Love: A Book of Remembrances*; and "6:35 a.m. to 7:35 a.m." from *Briefly*; all poems by permission of the author.

LOUIS DUDEK

b. 1918

The Pomegranate

The jewelled mine of the pomegranate, whose hexagons of
    honey
The mouth would soon devour but the eyes eat like a poem,
Lay hidden long in its hide, a diamond of dark cells
Nourished by tiny streams which crystallized into gems.

The seeds, nescient of the world outside, or of passionate
    teeth,
Prepared their passage into light and air, while tender roots
And branches dreaming in the cell-walled hearts of plants
Made silent motions such as recreate both men and fruits.

There, in a place of no light, shone that reddest blood,
And without a word of order, marshalled those grenadiers:
Gleaming without a sun—what art where no eyes were!—
Till broken by my hand, this palace of unbroken tears.

To wedding bells and horns howling down an alley,
Muffled, the married pair in closed caravan ride;
And then, the woman grown in secret, shining white,
Unclothed, mouth to mouth he holds his naked bride.

And there are days, golden days, when the world starts to life
When streets in the sun, boys, and battlefields of cars,
The colours on a bannister, the vendors' slanting stands
Send the pulse pounding on like the bursting of meteors—

As now, the fruit glistens with a mighty grin,
Conquers the room; and, though in ruin, to its death
Laughs at the light that wounds it, wonderfully red,
So that its awful beauty stops the greedy breath.

And can this fact be made, so big, of the body, then?
And is beauty bounded all in its impatient mesh?
The movement of the stars is that, and all their light
Secretly bathed the world, that now flows out of flesh.

FROM *Europe*

19

The commotion of these waves, however strong, cannot dis-
   turb
                     the compass-line of the horizon
nor the plumb-line of gravity, because this cross coordinates
                  the tragic pulls of necessity
that chart the ideal endings, for waves, and storms
                and sunset winds:
the dead scattered on the stage in the fifth act
—Cordelia in Lear's arms, Ophelia, Juliet, all silent—
show nature restored to order and just measure.
                    The horizon is perfect,
and nothing can be stricter
than gravity; in relation to these
             the stage is rocked and tossed,
kings fall with their crowns, poets sink with their laurels.

95

The sea retains such images
        in her ever-unchanging waves;
for all her infinite variety, and the forms,
inexhaustible, of her loves,
she is constant always in beauty,
           which to us need be nothing more
than a harmony with the wave on which we move.

All ugliness is a distortion
of the lovely lines and curves
                    which sincerity makes out of hands
                        and bodies moving in air.
Beauty is ordered in nature
                    as the wind and sea
shape each other for pleasure; as the just
know, who learn of happiness
                    from the report of their own actions.

Coming Suddenly to the Sea

Coming suddenly to the sea in my twenty-eighth year,
to the mother of all things that breathe, of mussels and
        whales,
I could not see anything but sand at first
and burning bits of mother-of-pearl.
But this was the sea, terrible as a torch
which the winter sun had lit,
flaming in the blue and salt sea-air
under my twenty-eight-year infant eyes.
And then I saw the spray smashing the rocks
and the angry gulls cutting the air,
the heads of fish and the hands of crabs on stones:
the carnivorous sea, sower of life,
battering a granite rock to make it a pebble—
love and pity needless as the ferny froth on its long smooth
        waves.
The sea, with its border of crinkly weed,
the inverted Atlantic of our unstable planet,
froze me into a circle of marble, sending the icy air out in
        lukewarm waves.
And so I brought home, as an emblem of that day
ending my long blind years, a fistful of blood-red weed in my
        hand.

The Jungle

Time has its ends and its beginnings—
    leaf-end and stems, skin and liver—
through which the rhythm passes,
    a drum-beat in a jungle silence,
somewhere in the trees the shriek
    of a wild bird shattered by claws,
somewhere the big cats mating, crying
    in pain, possibly in delight,
and the silence is endless, listening to the drums
    day after day with a new beginning,
day after day anguish, possibly pleasure,
    but beyond that the perfect white of the sky
waiting above the world for the movement to cease,
    to be absorbed in the folds of its sea,
to be drowned in space where all that was
    is sound in a deaf ear, fear in a forgotten dream.

FROM *Atlantis*

42

I seem to peer through time, as through a tottering mansion,
to glimpse the shapes beyond, the spectral bone-men
           who lived, and died, and believed.

And see the new religion fearfully replacing the old,
           burning temples,
knowing, past cure, how sure their reasons were
           against the old idols,
who now are burned themselves, with the sure fire of reason.

Nothing stands, we say, we moderns.
All's flux, an art of mathematics—of fiery matter,
while the old gods gutter and die in the flames.

45

I went to see one of the gods
                    still living
Ezra Pound
            by the Domus Aurea
in Rome, in the city of Propertius,
            of Marcus Valerius Martial

the greatest river god of them all

dying, in a great bed, into immortality
                    like those other ruins
(yet thin, and beautiful as youth)
that once were pillared in marble form
            by the sacred wood of arches

And he said...
        well, nothing
Only the tears filled his eyes
        as the great heart beat badly

And I walked around that place a little, and went my way.

96

There, somewhere, at the horizon
                    you cannot tell the sea from the sky,
where the white cloud glimmers,

the only reality, in a sea of unreality,

out of that cloud come palaces, and domes,
                            and marble capitals,
and carvings of ivory and gold—
                            Atlantis
shines invisible, in that eternal cloud.

Autumn

All day the leaves have been falling.
  thought of snow,
but the ground is covered with yellow meal
              that you can put your foot through
as you go walking, in an eternal still.

Soft as air the dry leaves,
and the dried weed at my doorstep
              a thorny bone as beautiful
as the shape of anything when seen alone.

It is all quite dead and finished,'
        you say, as you walk between houses and trees
holding your breath in mild wonder
              at seeing the ghost you will become.

Life & Art

She sings, sweet in all the streets,
        soft as a nocturnal love in arms,
with clashing colors, brazen breasts, hatless heads.
And if she won't, let her whistle off somewhere,
              let him be, first,
twisting onwards — life
              first, and art after, if a choice
                    must be made.
Because she stinks, the old witch, when the demon
              fact has not loved her
up-in-air, a beautiful belly-of-a-girl.
And he is all goat without her by him ambling.

AL PURDY

b. 1918

The Country North of Belleville

Bush land scrub land—
  Cashel Township and Wollaston
Elzevir McClure and Dungannon
green lands of Weslemkoon Lake
where a man might have some
  opinion of what beauty
is and none deny him
    for miles—

 Yet this is the country of defeat
where Sisyphus rolls a big stone
year after year up the ancient hills
picnicking glaciers have left strewn
with centuries' rubble
    backbreaking days
    in the sun and rain
when realization seeps slow in the mind
without grandeur or self deception in
    noble struggle
of being a fool—

A country of quiescence and still distance
a lean land
    not like the fat south
with inches of black soil on
    earth's round belly—
And where the farms are
    it's as if a man stuck
both thumbs in the stony earth and pulled

[Handwritten annotations in margins:]
used as a refrain — incantatory rhythm makes their magic.
ironic ref to lit. critics
honest sentiment
indicating living on the land is a somewhat futile existance.
look @ past affection for history & greek mythology — react to roll stone up hill for life eternity
self deprecating irony
Anti American

                              it apart
                              to make room
enough between the trees
for a wife
               and maybe some cows and
               room for some
of the more easily kept illusions—
And where the farms have gone back
to forest
               are only soft outlines
               shadowy differences—

Old fences drift vaguely among the trees
               a pile of moss-covered stones
gathered for some ghost purpose
has lost meaning under the meaningless sky   *20th Cent. phrase.*
          —they are like cities under water
and the undulating green waves of time
               are laid on them—

This is the country of our defeat   *Ref. to Canada? also to land? (farm)*
               and yet
during the fall plowing a man
might stop and stand in a brown valley of the furrows
               and shade his eyes to watch for the same
               red patch mixed with gold
               that appears on the same
               spot in the hills
               year after year
               and grow old
plowing and plowing a ten-acre field until
the convolutions run parallel with his own brain—

And this is a country where the young   *another aspect of imigrant status*
               leave quickly
unwilling to know what their fathers know
or think the words their mothers do not say—

Herschel Monteagle and Faraday
lakeland rockland and hill country

[handwritten: Not a global Nation]

a little adjacent to where the world is
a little north of where the cities are and
sometime
we may go back there
                              to the country of our defeat
Wollaston Elzevir and Dungannon
and Weslemkoon lake land
where the high townships of Cashel
                              McClure and Marmora once were—
But it's been a long time since
and we must enquire the way
              of strangers—

[handwritten: If you leave your region's then come back, you will find that everything has changed]

Necropsy of Love

If it came about you died
it might be said I loved you:
love is an absolute as death is,
and neither bears false witness to the other—
But you remain alive.

No, I do not love you
              hate the word,
that private tyranny inside a public sound,
your freedom's yours and not my own:
but hold my separate madness like a sword,
and plunge it in your body all night long.

If death shall strip our bones of all but bones,
then here's the flesh and flesh that's drunken-sweet
as wine cups in deceptive lunar light:
reach up your hand and turn the moonlight off,
and maybe it was never there at all,
so never promise anything to me:
but reach across the darkness with your hand,
reach across the distance of tonight,
and touch the moving moment once again
              before you fall asleep—

Song of the Impermanent Husband — Honest

Oh I would
I would in a minute
if the cusswords and bitter anger couldn't—
if the either/or quarrel didn't—
and the fat around my middle wasn't—
if I was young if
                    I wasn't so damn sure
I couldn't find another maddening bitch
like you holding on for dear life to
all the different parts of me for
twenty or twenty
                    thousand years
I'd leave in the night like
a disgraced caviar salesman
                    descend the moonlight
stairs to Halifax
                    (uh-no-not Halifax)
well then Toronto
                    ah
I guess not Toronto either/or
rain-soaked Vancouver down
                              down
                                    down
the dark stairs to
the South Seas' sunlit milky reefs and
            the jungle's green
                        unending bank account with
all the brown girls being brown
                    as they can be and all
the one piece behinds stretched tight tonight
in small sarongs gawd not to be touched tho Oh
beautiful as an angel's ass
—without the genitals
And me
        in Paris like a smudged Canadian postcard and
(dear me)
        all the importuning white and lily girls
of Rue Pigalle

                         and stroll
the sodden London streets and
                         find a sullen foggy woman who
enjoyed my odd colonial ways and send
a postcard back to you about my faithfulness and
talk about the lovely beastly English weather
I'd be the slimiest most uxorious wife deserter
                         my shrunk amoeba self absurd inside
a saffron girl's geography and
hating me between magnetic nipples
but
      fooling no one
in all the sad and much emancipated world
Why then I'll stay
                  at least for tea for
all the brownness is too brown and
all the whiteness too damned white
and I'm afraid
                  afraid of being
any other woman's man
who might be me
                  afraid
the unctuous and uneasy self I glimpse
sometimes might lose my faint and yapping cry
for being anything
                         was never quite what I intended
And you you
                  bitch no irritating
questions re love and permanence only
                  an unrolling lifetime here
between your rocking thighs

                  and the semblance of motion

The Cariboo Horses

At 100 Mile House the cowboys ride in rolling
stagey cigarettes with one hand reining
half-tame bronco rebels on a morning grey as stone
—so much like riding dangerous women
        with whiskey coloured eyes—
such women as once fell dead with their lovers
with fire in their heads and slippery froth on thighs
—Beaver or Carrier women maybe or
        Blackfoot squaws far past the edge of this valley
on the other side of those two toy mountain ranges
        from the sunfierce plains beyond

But only horses
            waiting in stables
hitched at taverns
              standing at dawn
pastured outside the town with
jeeps and fords and chevvys and
busy muttering stake trucks rushing
importantly over roads of man's devising
over the safe known roads of the ranchers
families and merchants of the town
        On the high prairie
are only horse and rider
        wind in dry grass
clopping in silence under the toy mountains
dropping sometimes and
        lost in the dry grass
        golden oranges of dung

Only horses
       no stopwatch memories or palace ancestors
not Kiangs hauling undressed stone in the Nile Valley
and having stubborn Egyptian tantrums or
Onagers racing thru Hither Asia and
the last Quagga screaming in African highlands

                    lost relatives of these
                    whose hooves were thunder
the ghosts of horses battering thru the wind
whose names were the wind's common usage
whose life was the sun's
                    arriving here at chilly noon
                    in the gasoline smell of the
                    dust and waiting 15 minutes
                    at the grocer's

Wilderness Gothic

Metaphor for Faith.

Across Roblin Lake, two shores away,
they are sheathing the church spire
with new metal. Someone hangs in the sky
over there from a piece of rope,
hammering and fitting God's belly-scratcher,
working his way up along the spire
until there's nothing left to nail on—
Perhaps the workman's faith reaches beyond:
touches intangibles, wrestles with Jacob,
replacing rotten timber with pine thews,
pounds hard in the blue cave of the sky,
contends heroically with difficult problems of
gravity, sky navigation and mythopeia,
his volunteer time and labour donated to God,
minus sick benefits of course on a non-union job—

Fields around are yellowing into harvest,
nestling and fingerling are sky and water borne,
death is yodelling quiet in green woodlots,
and bodies of three young birds have disappeared
in the sub-surface of the new county highway—

That picture is incomplete, part left out
that might alter the whole Dürer landscape:
gothic ancestors peer from medieval sky,
dour faces trapped in photograph albums escaping

to clop down iron roads with matched greys:
work-sodden wives groping inside their flesh
for what keeps moving and changing and flashing
beyond and past the long frozen Victorian day.
A sign of fire and brimstone? A two-headed calf
born in the barn last night? A sharp female agony?
An age and a faith moving into transition,
the dinner cold and new-baked bread a failure,
deep woods shiver and water drops hang pendant,
double yolked eggs and the house creaks a little—
Something is about to happen. Leaves are still.
Two shores away, a man hammering in the sky.
Perhaps he will fall.

Elegy for a Grandfather

Well, he died I guess. They said he did.
His wide whalebone hips will make a prehistoric barrow
men of the future may find and perhaps may not:
where this man's relatives ducked their heads
in real and pretended sorrow
for the dearly beloved gone thank Christ to God,
after a bad century: a tough big-bellied Pharaoh,
with a deck of cards in his pocket and a Presbyterian grin—

Maybe he did die, but the boy didn't understand it;
the man knows now and the scandal never grows old
of a happy lumberjack who lived on rotten whiskey,
and died of sin and Quaker oats age 90 or so.
But all he was was too much for any man to be,
a life so full he couldn't include one more thing,
nor tell the same story twice if he'd wanted to,
and didn't and didn't—

Just the same he's dead. A sticky religious voice
folded his century sideways to get it out of sight,
and lowered him into the ground like someone still alive
who made other people uncomfortable:

barn raiser and backwoods farmer,
become an old man in a one-room apartment
over a drygoods store—
And earth takes him as it takes more beautiful things:
populations of whole countries,
museums and works of art,
and women with such a glow
it makes their background vanish
                         they vanish too,
and Lesbos' singer in her sunny islands
stopped when the sun went down—

No, my grandfather was decidedly unbeautiful,
250 pounds of scarred slag.
And I've somehow become his memory,
taking on flesh and blood again
the way he imagined me,
floating among the pictures in his mind
where his dead body is,
laid deep in the earth—
and such a relayed picture perhaps
outlives any work of art,
survives among its alternatives.

Eskimo Graveyard

Walking in glacial litter
frost boils and boulder pavements
of an old river delta
where angry living water
changes its mind every half century
and takes a new direction
to the blue fiord
The Public Works guy I'm with
says you always find good gravel
for concrete near a graveyard

where digging is easy maybe
a footnote on human character
But wrapped in blankets
above ground a dead old woman
(for the last few weeks I'm told)
without a grave marker
And a hundred yards away
the Anglican missionary's grave
with whitewashed cross
that means equally nothing
The river's soft roar
drifts to my ears and changes
tone when the wind changes
ice debris melts at low tide
& the Public Works guy is mildly pleased
with the good gravel we found
for work on the schoolhouse
which won't have to be shipped in
from Montreal
and mosquitoes join happily
in our conversation   Then
he stops to consult
with the construction foreman
I walk on
towards the tents of The People
half a mile away
at one corner of the picture
Mothers with children on their backs
in the clean white parkas
they take such pride in
buying groceries at H.B.C.
boys lounging under the store
in space where timber stilts
hold it above the permafrost
with two of them arm in arm
in the manner of Eskimo friends
After dinner
I walk down among the tents
and happen to think of the old woman

neither wholly among the dead
nor quite gone from the living
and wonder how often
a thought of hers enters the minds
of people she knew before
and what kind of flicker it is
as lights begin to come on
in nightlong twilight
and thoughts of me
occur to the mosquitoes
I keep walking
as if something ought to happen
(I don't know what)
with the sun stretching
a yellow band across the water
from headland to black headland
at high tide in the fiord
sealing in the settlement
as if there was no way out
and indeed there isn't
until the looping Cansos come
dropping thru the mountain doorway
That old woman?
it occurs to me
I might have been thinking
about human bookkeeping
debits and credits that is
or profit and loss
(and laugh at myself)
among the sealed white tents
like glowing swans
hoping
for a most improbable
birth

PANGNIRTUNG

Trees at the Arctic Circle

(SALIX CORDIFOLIA — GROUND WILLOW)

They are 18 inches long
or even less
crawling under rocks
grovelling among the lichens
bending and curling to escape
making themselves small
finding new ways to hide
Coward trees
I am angry to see them
like this
not proud of what they are
bowing to weather instead
careful of themselves
worried about the sky
afraid of exposing their limbs
like a Victorian married couple

[handwritten margin notes: — Ref. To Cad. Identity — cowards, always sorry — 100 yrs out of Date]

I call to mind great Douglas firs
I see tall maples waving green
and oaks like gods in autumn gold
the whole horizon jungle dark
and I crouched under that continual night
But these
even the dwarf shrubs of Ontario
mock them
Coward trees
And yet — and yet —
their seed pods glow
like delicate grey earrings
their leaves are veined and intricate
like tiny parkas
They have about three months
to make sure the species does not die

and that's how they spend their time
unbothered by any human opinion
just digging in here and now
sending their roots down down down
And you know it occurs to me
                    about 2 feet under
those roots must touch permafrost
ice that remains ice forever
and they use it for their nourishment
they use death to remain alive

I see that I've been carried away
in my scorn of the dwarf trees
most foolish in my judgments
To take away the dignity
                    of any living thing
even tho it cannot understand
                    the scornful words
is to make life itself trivial
and yourself the Pontifex Maximus   *chief judge*
                    of nullity   *of nothing*
I have been stupid in a poem
I will not alter the poem
but let the stupidity remain permanent
as the trees are
in a poem
the dwarf trees of Baffin Island

PANGNIRTUNG

Lament for the Dorsets

(ESKIMOS EXTINCT IN THE 14TH CENTURY A.D.)

Animal bones and some mossy tent rings
scrapers and spearheads   carved ivory swans
all that remains of the Dorset giants
who drove the Vikings back to their long ships
talked to spirits of earth and water

—a picture of terrifying old men
so large they broke the backs of bears
so small they lurk behind bone rafters
in the brain of modern hunters
among good thoughts and warm things
and come out at night
to spit on the stars

The big men with clever fingers
who had no dogs and hauled their sleds
over the frozen northern oceans
awkward giants
                killers of seal
they couldn't compete with little men
who came from the west with dogs
Or else in a warm climatic cycle
the seals went back to cold waters
and the puzzled Dorsets scratched their heads
with hairy thumbs around 1350 A.D.
—couldn't figure it out
went around saying to each other
plaintively
           "What's wrong? What happened?
           Where are the seals gone?"
And died

Twentieth century people
apartment dwellers
executives of neon death
warmakers with things that explode
—they have never imagined us in their future
how could we imagine them in the past
squatting among the moving glaciers
six hundred years ago
with glowing lamps?
As remote or nearly
as the trilobites and swamps
when coal became

or the last great reptile hissed
at a mammal the size of a mouse
that squeaked and fled

Did they ever realize at all
what was happening to them?
Some old hunter with one lame leg
a bear had chewed
sitting in a caribou-skin tent
—the last Dorset?
Let's say his name was Kudluk
and watch him sitting there
carving 2-inch ivory swans
for a dead grand-daughter
taking them out of his mind
the places in his mind
where pictures are
He selects a sharp stone tool
to gouge a parallel pattern of lines
on both sides of the swan
holding it with his left hand
bearing down and transmitting
his body's weight
from brain to arm and right hand
and one of his thoughts
turns to ivory
The carving is laid aside
in beginning darkness
at the end of hunger
and after a while wind
blows down the tent and snow
begins to cover him

After 600 years
the ivory thought
is still warm

The Road to Newfoundland

My foot has pushed a fire ahead of me
for a thousand miles
my arms' response to hills and stones
has stated parallel green curves
deep in my unknown country
the clatter of gravel on fenders registers
on a ghostly player piano
inside my head with harsh fraying music
I'm lost to reality
but turn the steering wheel a quarter
inch to avoid a bug on the road
A long time's way here since stone
age man carried the fire-germ
in a moss-lined basket
from camp to camp
and prayed to it
as I shall solemnly hold Henry Ford
and all his descendants accountable
to the 24,000 mile guarantee
Well there are many miles left
before it expires and several
more to the next rest
stop and I kick the fire
ahead of me with one foot
even harder than before
hearing the sound of burning
forests muffled in steel
toppling buildings
history accelerating
racing up and down
hills with my flesh grown captive
of a steel extension of myself
hauling down the sun and stars
for mileposts going nowhere fast
wanting speed and more Speed

—Stop
at a calm lake
embossed with 2-inch waves
sit there a few minutes
without getting out of the car
my heart a hammering drum
among the trees' and grass roots'
August diminuendo
watching the composed landscape
the sun where it's supposed to be
in its deliberate dance thru space
then drive steadily north
with the captive fire
in cool evening
towards the next camp

Inside the Mill

It's a building where men are still working
thru sunlight and starlight and moonlight
despite the black holes plunging down
on their way to the roots of the earth
no danger exists for them
transparent as shadows they labour
in their manufacture of light

I've gone there lonely sometimes
the way I felt as a boy
and something lightened inside me
—old hands sift the dust that was flour
and the lumbering wagons returning
afloat in their pillar of shadows
as the great wheel turns the world

When you cross the doorway you feel them
when you cross the places they've been
there's a flutter of time in your heartbeat
of time going backward and forward
if you feel it and perhaps you don't
but it's voyaging backward and forward
on a gate in the sea of your mind

When the mill was torn down I went back there
birds fumed into fire at the place
a red sun beat hot in the stillness
they moved there transparent as morning
one illusion balanced another
as the dream holds the real in proportion
and the howl in our hearts to a sigh

RAYMOND SOUSTER

b. 1921

Where the Blue Horses

The street is quiet,
any noise through the wall is stilled,
our little cat curled up on the kitchen chair,
the radio finally off,
milk bottles placed outside the door.

So for now
nothing but sleep and dreams and thoughts of sleep,
not even love keeps us awake tonight,

as we sink into that strange land
where the blue horses toss
riderless and proud.

Yonge Street Saturday Night

Except when the theatre crowds engulf the sidewalks
at nine, at eleven-thirty,
this street is lonely, and a thousand lights
in a thousand store windows
wouldn't break her lips into a smile.

There are a few bums out,
there are lovers with hands held tightly,
there are also the drunk ones
but they are princes among men, and are few.

And there are some like us,
just walking, making both feet move out ahead of us,
a little bored, a little lost, a little angry,

walking as though we were honestly going somewhere,
walking as if there was really something to see
at Adelaide or maybe on King,
something, no matter how little
that will give us some fair return
on our use of shoe-leather,

something perhaps that will make us smile
with a strange new happiness,
a lost but recovered joy.

Downtown Corner Newsstand

It will take death to move you from this corner,
for it's become your world and you its unshaved,
bleary-eyed, foot-stamping king.

In winter you curse the cold, huddled in your coat from the
        wind,
then fry in summer like an egg hopping in a pan,
and always that whining voice, those nervous-flinging arms,
the red face, shifting eyes watching, waiting
under the grimy cap for God knows what to happen.

But nothing ever does; downtown Toronto
goes to sleep and wakes the next morning
always the same, except a little dirtier,
as you stand with your armful of *Stars* and *Telys*,
the peak of your cap well down against the sun,
and all the city's restless, seething river
surges up around you, but never once
do you plunge in its flood to be carried or tossed away—

but reappear always, beard longer than ever, nose running,
to catch the noon editions at King and Bay.

Two Dead Robins

In the driveway, their bodies so small
I almost stepped on them, two baby robins,
enormous mouths, bulging eyes, bodies thin wire
stretched over taut skin frames, bones showing
like aroused veins.
                    It looked as though they'd either
tried to fly from the nest above
or the wind had swept them down. For some reason
I couldn't bear to pick them up in my hands,
so got a spade and buried them quickly
at the back of the garden, thinking as I did it

how many will die today, have much worse burial
than these two my shovel mixes under?

Study: The Bath

In the dim light
of the bathroom
a woman steps from white tub,
towel around her shoulders.

Drops of water glisten
on her body
from slight buttocks,
neck, tight belly,
fall at intervals
from the slightly plumed
oval of crotch.

The neck bent forward,
eyes collected,
her attention gathered
at the end of fingers,

lovingly removing
dead, flaked skin
from the twin nipples.

Armadale Avenue Revisited

Street of my boyhood
(I lived right around the corner),
quiet, leaf-heavy street
of West Toronto.
                Here,
behind that house, in the lane,
from garage roofs we ambushed
the Nelles Street gang,
pinned them down with catapults,
then, out of acorns,
forgot all our strategy
and ran like hell.
                Out this door
on Christmas Day
of all days, that queer girl
came sleep-walking, nightgown and all,
and even the snow underfoot
couldn't waken her.
                At this number lived
the grease-monkey boys,
(their Stutz Touring shined
to a blinding dazzle),
who sometimes took me
as heart-pounding passenger
out the Queen Elizabeth,
to run her, gun her
past eighty on a straight stretch,
with the extra spice
of maybe a speed-cop
coming out of nowhere.
                On this lawn
I pounded and bloodied
my next-to-worst enemy,
and curiously found
it wasn't fun anymore....

But tonight it's only
ghosts I see around these houses,
the old gang gone,
every one of them;
some killed in war,
some from natural causes,
the rest, I can guess,
growing fat and middle-aged
like me.
       But not one of them
comes back here, I know,
they've got better sense:

just the crazy poet
well hooked on the past,
a sucker for memories.

Pigeons on George Street

As I draw abreast of him
the stranger draws from his leather pouch
handfuls of feed-grain which he sprinkles
half on the sidewalk, half at the curb,
next, slices of dried bread which he breaks
and scatters just as carefully:
                    while across
the street and above on the tight-rope wire
of the telephone lines at least a hundred pigeons
burn with the desire to flutter down, attack
the daily handout.
            But no-one moves,
and my new friend says, "There's too much traffic
on the street today for them, they'll all sit tight
until things quiet down."
              And he's right:
when I look down the street
five minutes later, one hundred pigeons

are still up there on the wires, and only half a dozen
braver (hungrier?) sparrows busy eating.

Which for no good reason I can think of
gives me the curious feeling that long, long after
the last pigeon has flapped off the earth,
the sparrows, if they have their way,
will still be with us.

ELI MANDEL

b. 1922

Notes from the Underground

A woman built herself a cave
    and furnished it with torn machines
    and tree-shaped trunks and dictionaries.
Out of the town where she sprang
    to her cave of rusting texts and springs
    rushed fables of indifferent rape
    and children slain indifferently
    and daily blood.

Would you believe how free I have become
    with lusting after her?
                    That I have become
    a melodramatist, my friends ashamed?

I have seen by the light of her burning texts
    how the indifferent blood drips
    from the brass mouths of my friends,
    how at the same table I have supped
    and grown fat.

Her breasts are planets in a reedy slough.
Lie down beside that slough awhile
    and taste the bitter reeds.

Read in the water how a drowning man
    sings of a free green life.

Marina

Because she spoke often of the sea we thought she had
   known another country, her people distant, not
   forgotten

We did not know then who was calling her or what songs
   she listened to or why the sea-birds came to rest
   upon her long fingers

Or why she would shudder like a sea-bird about to take
   flight, her eyes changing with the changing light

As the sea-changing opal changes, as a shell takes its
   colours from the sea as if it were the sea

As if the great sea itself were held in the palm of your hand

They say the daughters of the sea know the language of
      birds,
   that in their restless eyes the most fortunate learn
   how the moon rises and sets

We do not know who is calling her or why her eyes change
   or what shore she will set her foot upon

Agatha Christie

being civil she saw poison
as a flaw in character
the use of a knife
a case history in Freud

difficult to explain
her dislike of jews

or why night upon night
she plotted solutions
to deaths she must have dreamed

her 200,000,000 readers
how much longing for murder
the neatness of England
is and still remains

though in Belfast, say,
bombs have other reasons
and no one explains

Earthworms Eat Earthworms and Learn

as with Aunt Adeline
the one with the large bosom
one of my complicated cousins
who on a hot Regina afternoon
wept at a hurt finger
and thrust into her vagina
other fingers

so eating one another worm
knows inside another worm
the square root Adeline knew
and cousins knowing cousins
uncles uncles
aunts aunts

it goes on
wisdom of cells

this rod dividing into that
rod into that code that code

so it was with Aunt Eda
who coded Uncle Lou
who had himself been coded

into

and father knew father
mothering the last of the jews
who on the Hirsch land
put in new seeds
and new codes
and new aunts

so we survived
but had become
being as
we were

solutions

the seed

the new seed

final solution

remember forever the neon
Orpheum (?) Winnipeg 1935
lights exploding liquid
oh the elegant lobby
uncles and lights lights lights
then
     film

estevan, 1934:

        remembering the family we
        called breeds   the Roques
        their house smelling of urine
        my mother's prayers before
        the dried fish she cursed
        them for their dirtiness their

women I remember too

                   how

seldom they spoke and
they touched one another

even when the sun killed
cattle and rabbis

                even

in poisoned slow air
like hunters

         like lizards

they touched   stone
they touched

         earth

birthmark:

seeing a mouse
my mother struck her temple

he'll be marked at birth
she said

        the women cried

I carry the souris
on my brow

        the river

in my head

        the valley

of my dreams
still echoes
with her cry

the double world:

it is variously believed that this world is the
double of another, as in Plato, Swedenborg,
    Malebranche,
some of Immanuel Kant, Arthur C. Clarke, Isaac
    Asimov,
Stanley Kubrick
             Two clocks set at the same time in
identical universes should stop at the same time.
This clock is a shadow of that real clock. When I
    look at my clock I have no way of knowing
    whether I am in
the first or second universe. It is spring there too:
and the other Ann has grown an avocado exactly
    the same
height, greenness, number of leaves as the one
    Ann grew
here or there. My grandfather Berner weighed the
    same
in both universes, sang sweet Jewish psalms, ate
    sour
curds. In the two graveyards Annie Berner is
    dead.
Nothing on either prairie changes though the
    winds blow
across immensities your heart would shrivel to
    imagine
knowing they pass between the worlds and can be
    heard to do
so on the road to Wood Mountain. That is what
    was written
in the rocks.

"Grandfather's Painting": David Thauberger

Under David Thauberger's painting
showing his grandfather's house
and that giant horse standing above it,
the town of Holdfast, wheat fields,
church, elevators, and prairie grass
the TV set turned to a
Saturday Night Movie called "Marathon Man"
looks very small and peculiar,
but the movie is about politics,
betrayal and South American Nazis: it has to do
with various kinds of torture,
the use of a dentist's drill,
for example, the tyranny of McCarthy
in America of the fifties, Jews,
their memory, camps, the White Angel,
specialist in teeth, skulls, and diamonds.
        You wouldn't believe how large the horse is
in Thauberger's painting above the TV set
and yet it only portrays a symbol of how his grandfather
ruled the land, the power by which the little town
was run, the motor of the little town called Holdfast
while beneath it the real powers that run us,
pictures, say, and how we know how to kill one another,
metaphors of murder, these are played out night
upon night and I watch them and watch the painting,
no longer knowing whether I should write poetry,
especially poems about land, about Estevan,
or about why I came back to Regina, Saskatchewan,
this cold winter of 1979 or what I thought
I might find in a city of this kind to write of,
now that my father is dead for many years, and my mother,
and most of my friends are in the arts

There are nights
old enough to kill. They remind me of my boyhood,
how much I loved the winter on the prairies, never
believing it was deadly or that we fought to be alive here
though my fantasies were of war. That powerful animal,
this evening with the Marathon Man running,
running, I suddenly know David was right to paint him,
his grandfather. We stand over the land, fathers,
and over our homes and over each other.
We have terrible forces inside us: we can paint them,
green, acrylic, glitter: the form never lies.
The truth is in the long dead winters where we live.

Parting at Udaipur: the Lake Palace

In Calcutta a Bengali artist explains
his family lived in a tree swarming with uncles
incest and possession. It is an allegory.
Then there's the other story about a mongoose mother.
The tree swarms. Later his mother
will warn him she is about to die.

I think of snake charmers, how they produce
out of a sack a blur of slither
and how it clamps teeth into a python's head,
savaging the dull beast.

At Gujarat an intellectual lets me know
she despises her husband, academics, poetry
her unequivocal dark hands handling a book,
poems my friend has given her.

From the Taj windows in Bombay
the Gates of India imperial and aloof
open to the Arabian sea. The heat drains
whatever leans in the wind that blows from the desert.
The harbour fills with the blood of the setting sun.

I despair of reason, knowledge, my lectures,
remember only Ann turning away at Udaipur,
the boat from the palace creating distances.
We are in a strange land. We are drifting apart.
India is between us. Across the lake, its sunken
woman, lie continents:

>   war   torture   poison
>   an apparatus of romance
>   to keep us apart.

In My 57th Year

This is the year my mother lay dying
knocked down by tiny strokes she claimed
never once hit her though when she lay
crib-like where they laid her there she wept
for shame to be confined so near her death.
This is the year the cancer inside my father's
groin began its growth to knock him down
strong as he was beside his stricken wife.
This is the year I grew, ignorant of politics,
specious with law, careless of poetry.
There were no graves. The prairie rolled on
as if it were the sea. Today my children make
their way alone across those waves.
Do lines between us end as sharply
as lines our artists draw upon the plains?
I cry out. They keep their eye upon
their politics, their myths,
careful of lives as I was careless.

What shall I say? It is too late to tell again
tales we never knew. The legends of ourselves
spill into silence. All we never said, father
to daughter, son to unmanned man, we cannot say
to count the years.
>   I no longer know time or age
thinking of parents, their time, their grave of names.
Telling the time, fiction consumes me.

MILTON ACORN

b. 1923

Charlottetown Harbor

An old docker with gutted cheeks,
time arrested in the used-up-knuckled hands
crossed on his lap, sits
in a spell of the glinting water.

He dreams of times in the cider sunlight
when masts stood up like stubble;
but now a gull cries, lights,
flounces its wings ornately, folds them,
and the waves slop among the weed-grown piles.

The Island

Since I'm Island-born home's as precise
as if a mumbly old carpenter,
shoulder-straps crossed wrong,
laid it out,
refigured to the last three-eighths of shingle.

Nowhere that plow-cut worms
heal themselves in red loam;
spruces squat, skirts in sand;
or the stones of a river rattle its dark
tunnel under the elms,
is there a spot not measured by hands;
no direction I couldn't walk
to the wave-lined edge of home.

In the fanged jaws of the Gulf,
a red tongue.
Indians say a musical God
took up his brush and painted it;
named it, in His own language,
"The Island."

I've Tasted My Blood

If this brain's over-tempered
consider that the fire was want
and the hammers were fists.
I've tasted my blood too much
to love what I was born to.

But my mother's look
was a field of brown oats, soft-bearded;
her voice rain and air rich with lilacs:
and I loved her too much to like
how she dragged her days like a sled over gravel.

Playmates? I remember where their skulls roll!
One died hungry, gnawing grey porch-planks;
one fell, and landed so hard he splashed;
and many and many
come up atom by atom
in the worm-casts of Europe.

My deep prayer a curse.
My deep prayer the promise that this won't be.
My deep prayer my cunning,
my love, my anger,
and often even my forgiveness
that this won't be and be.
I've tasted my blood too much
to abide what I was born to.

The Idea

It's events itch the idea
into existence. The clawing
pixilating world lofts
the mind and its wrangling images
as contrary, gusty, circling
winds toss, flaunt the flags
(splendrous as if living) of
old duchies, unforgotten empires.

Then something palpable as voltage,
maybe a grim preacher, maybe
a wild thin man on a soapbox,
or even a character lugging
a pail and whitewash brush
(whitewash or smear it's all
a point of view) takes charge:
something you want in a way
savage or happy, takes charge:
the idea grows flesh, with nerves
to feel the pain of dismemberment.

But its life is death, and life's
going back to the chewing
creation obeying just itself;
so the herded clouds, dream-beasts
in the eyes' pasture, are torn
to fall like tears, like blood.
Then the idea's more like blood,
something in time with running feet,
with typewriter, with heartbeat.

Knowing I Live in a Dark Age

Knowing I live in a dark age before history,
I watch my wallet and
am less struck by gunfights in the avenues
than by the newsie with his dirty pink chapped face
calling a shabby poet back for his change.

The crows mobbing the blinking, sun-stupid owl;
wolves eating a hamstrung calf hindend first,
keeping their meat alive and fresh . . . these
are marks of foresight, beginnings of wit:
but Jesus wearing thorns and sunstroke
beating his life and death into words
to break the rods and blunt the axes of Rome:
this and like things followed.

Knowing that in this advertising rainbow
I live like a trapeze artist with a headache,
my poems are no aspirins . . . they show
pale bayonets of grass waving thin on dunes;
the paralytic and his lyric secrets;
my friend Al, union builder and cynic,
hesitating to believe his own delicate poems
lest he believe in something better than himself:
and history, which is yet to begin,
will exceed this, exalt this
as a poem erases and rewrites its poet.

Poem for the Astronauts

As a wild duck painted sunrise colors
blurs his wings with speed
to a land known only to his heart's thrill
so man's truest home is the wind
created of his breath
and he breathes deepest in mystery.

New stars. Figures in the heavens.
Voices. How full
must be the vessel, the eye
that searches emptiness!

Canada is the scent of pines.
I left my land and returned
to know this and become Canadian.
To be an earthman I must leave Earth:
And what is Earth?
The whisper of grass?

Seeds turbulent
with fearful exultance
voyaging...

An Indian running the desert
kept a stone under his tongue
to drink the saliva, and
his skin remembered a thousand light touches
—fingers of his beloved.

The Natural History of Elephants

In the elephant's five-pound brain
The whole world's both table and shithouse
Where he wanders seeking viandes, exchanging great farts
For compliments. The rumble of his belly
Is like the contortions of a crumpling planetary system.
Long has he roved, his tongue longing to press the juices
From the ultimate berry, large as
But tenderer and sweeter than a watermelon;
And he leaves such signs in his wake that pygmies have fallen
And drowned in his great fragrant marshes of turds.

In the elephant's five-pound brain
The wind is diverted by the draughts of his breath,
Rivers are sweet gulps, and the ocean
After a certain distance is too deep for wading.
The earth is trivial, it has the shakes
And must be severely tested, else
It'll crumble into unsteppable clumps and scatter off
Leaving the great beast bellowing among the stars.

In the elephant's five-pound brain
Dwarves have an incredible vicious sincerity,
A persistent will to undo things. The beast cannot grasp
The convolutions of destruction, always his mind
Turns to other things—the vastness of green
And of frangibility of forest. If only once he could descend
To trivialities he'd sweep the whole earth clean of his
      tormentors
In one sneeze so mighty as to be observed from Mars.

In the elephant's five-pound brain
Sun and moon are the pieces in a delightfully complex
      ballgame
That have to do with him . . never does he doubt
The sky has opened and rain and thunder descend
For his special ministration. He dreams of mastodons
And mammoths and still his pride beats

Like the heart of the world, he knows he could reach
To the end of space if he stood still and imagined the effort.

In the elephant's five-pound brain
Poems are composed as a silent substitute for laughter,
His thoughts while resting in the shade
Are long and solemn as novels and he knows his companions
By names differing for each quality of morning.
Noon and evening are ruminated on and each overlaid
With the taste of night. He loves his horny perambulating
          hide
As other tribes love their houses, and remembers
He's left flakes of skin and his smell
As a sign and permanent stamp on wherever he has been.

In the elephant's five-pound brain
The entire Oxford dictionary'ld be too small
To contain all the concepts which after all are too weighty
Each individually ever to be mentioned;
Thus of course the beast has no language
Only an eternal pondering hesitation.

In the elephant's five-pound brain
The pliable trunk's a continuous diversion
That in his great innocence he never thinks of as perverse,
The pieces of the world are handled with such a thrilling
Tenderness that all his hours
Are consummated and exhausted with love.
Not slow to mate every female bull and baby
Is blessed with a gesture grandly gracious and felt lovely
Down to the sensitive great elephant toenails.

And when his more urgent pricking member
Stabs him on its horrifying season he becomes
A blundering mass of bewilderment . . . No thought
But twenty tons of lust he fishes madly for whales
And spiders to rape them. Sperm falls in great gouts
And the whole forest is sticky, colonies of ants
Are nourished for generations on dried elephant semen.

In the elephant's five-pound brain
Death is accorded no belief and old friends
Are continually expected, patience
Is longer than the lives of glaciers and the centuries
Are rattled like toy drums. A life is planned
Like a brush-stroke on the canvas of eternity,
And the beginning of a damnation is handled
With great thought as to its middle and its end.

Words Said Sitting on a Rock Sitting on a Saint

(IN MEMORIAM: RED LANE)

I

He had a way of stopping the light
, making it mark his darkness,
and a depth like a sounding line
played out, swinging its futile
weight far above bottom
, drank all his surfaces.

WARNING . . . Don't tempt the gods
with too much patience, for he poked
for poems as in the sand for stones
—round firm things, with no entrances

: and would wait for the end
of the time he was in, for
that discovery, the moment of vision
that for him was hard, like a stone

: and I reached out tendrils of thought
towards him . . . If he told me what a flower
was to him, I'd tell him what a flower
was to me. Thus we worked on each other,
patiently, as if each was immortal.

His dying is like an infinite grey sphere
of nothingness to the left hand of my sun,
and sometimes I draw the nothingness down
to wrap about me, like a cloak with a hood.

II

The saint of stone silences
is dead. The miracle is
that he does not speak,
even as when he made his sparing
moves in our game, his speakings
were flint fragments of no language,
harder silences.

The miracle is that the Earth still traces
all the circles of her whirling dance,
and those yo-yos of the sun, the comets
still comb their white curly hair
across the heavens, while he
as in life consents to all their courses.

Doomed to his time, he accepted it
and made a gnomic utterance of it. Caught on it
across, like a bow on a fiddle string
he drew the one note it was meant to say
by his agency, and concluded it
with the quietness that was its continuation.

In Memory of Joe En Lai
1898-1976
(THE CHINESE 'CHOU' IS PRONOUNCED 'JOE')

Never close the door on a parting friend.
Most inauspicious—that: hinting an end.
Watch him clear as he goes down the lane;
Photons from your eyes like a rain
Of blessings and good wishes. Hum
And memorize a song in his name
Which you'll hold secret til he comes again.

Never give a sign it's over and done.
Greet every new friend partly for his sake;
Thinking of him as just now gone and due back soon;
And if he doesn't return let loose that tune
To find and call him back wherever he's run.
Remember him behind in time, dream of him ahead.
Follow these instructions—even if he's dead.

Invocation

You loved one, hurt one, loving one still strong...
If you were only an impossible vision
Why would you lurk—a quiet worm in my tongue
Wait and live to raise this invocation?
What did you look through, in Spook Canyon
Besides that smiling mask, carved from a tree—
Tools learning as they cut a growing wisdom
To top and ornament your poor wronged body?
You have entered me, dead but not done.

I've loved, and love the Earth. If you are Death
Stay around to summon more performance.
Is that smile kinder yet? Plumbing consent?
Wait for the laughter! It'll blow breath
Tumbling all your atoms to collect 'em
Til lungs pump, your heart flutters, eyes go wide
And I'll be wise, at last, to find a bride.
My vehicle accelerates, bright one. Come.

JAMES REANEY

---

b. 1926

Antichrist as a Child

When Antichrist was a child
He caught himself tracing
The capital letter A
On a window sill
And wondered why
Because his name contained no A.
And as he crookedly stood
In his mother's flower-garden
He wondered why she looked so sadly
Out of an upstairs window at him.
He wondered why his father stared so
Whenever he saw his little son
Walking in his soot-coloured suit.
He wondered why the flowers
And even the ugliest weeds
Avoided his fingers and his touch.
And when his shoes began to hurt
Because his feet were becoming hooves
He did not let on to anyone
For fear they would shoot him for a monster.
He wondered why he more and more
Dreamed of eclipses of the sun,
Of sunsets, ruined towns and zeppelins,
And especially inverted, upside down churches.

The Red Heart

The only leaf upon its tree of blood,
My red heart hangs heavily
And will never fall loose,
But grow so heavy
After only a certain number of seasons
(Sixty winters, and fifty-nine falls,
Fifty-eight summers, and fifty-seven springs)
That it will bring bough
Tree and the fences of my bones
Down to a grave in the forest
Of my still upright fellows.

So does the sun hang now
From a branch of Time
In this wild fall sunset.
Who shall pick the sun
From the tree of Eternity?
Who shall thresh the ripe sun?
What midwife shall deliver
The Sun's great heir?
It seems that no one can,
And so the sun shall drag
Gods, goddesses and parliament buildings,
Time, Fate, gramaphones and Man
To a gray grave
Where all shall be trampled
Beneath the dancing feet of crowds
Of other still-living suns and stars.

The Royal Visit

When the King and the Queen came to Stratford
Everyone felt at once
How heavy the Crown must be.
The Mayor shook hands with their Majesties
And everyone presentable was presented
And those who weren't have resented
It, and will
To their dying day.
Everyone had almost a religious experience
When the King and Queen came to visit us
(I wonder what they felt!)
And hydrants flowed water in the gutters
All day.
People put quarters on the railroad tracks
So as to get squashed by the Royal Train
And some people up the line at Shakespeare
Stayed in Shakespeare, just in case—
They did stop too,
While thousands in Stratford
Didn't even see them
Because the Engineer didn't slow down
Enough in time.
And although,
But although we didn't see them in any way
(I didn't even catch the glimpse
The teacher who was taller did
Of a gracious pink figure)
I'll remember it to my dying day.

April Eclogue

ARGUMENT

With Duncan as judge the geese hold a bardic contest in
    honour of Spring.

DUNCAN RAYMOND VALANCY

Here is a kernel of the hardest winter wheat
Found in the yard delicious for to eat.
It I will give to that most poetic gander
Who this season sings as well as swam Leander.
The white geese with their orange feet on the green
Grass that grew round the pony'd glassy sheen
Chose then Valancy and Raymond to sing
And to hear them gathered about in a ring.

Raymond
I speak I speak of the arable earth,
Black sow goddess huge with birth;
Cry cry killdeers in her fields.

Black ogress ate her glacier lover
When the sun killed him for her;
The white owl to the dark crow yields.

Caw caw whir whir bark bark
We're fresh out of Noah's Ark;
Wild geese come in arrowheads

Shot from birds dead long ago
Buried in your negro snow;
Long water down the river sleds.

Black begum of a thousand dugs,
A nation at each fountain tugs;
The forests plug their gaps with leaves.

Whet whet scrape and sharpen
Hoes and rakes and plows of iron;
The farmer sows his sheaves.

Mr. Sword or Mr. Plow
Can settle in your haymow,
All is the same to Mother Ground.

Great goddess I from you have come,
Killdeer crow geese ditch leaf plowman
From you have come, to you return
In endless laughing weeping round.

Valancy
Your limbs are the rivers of Eden.
From the dead we see you return and arise,
Fair girl, lost daughter:
The swallows stream through the skies
Down dipping water,
Skimming ground, and from chimney's foul dusk
Their cousins the swifts tumble up as the tusk
Of roar day
In bright May
Scatters them gliding from darkness to sun-cusp.

Your face unlocks the bear from his den.
The world has come into the arms of the sun.
What now sulky earth?
All winter you lay with your face like a nun,
But now bring forth
From river up boxdrain underground
Fish crawling up that dark street without sound
To spawn
In our pond
Young suckers and sunfish within its deep round.

Your body is a bethlehem.
Come near the sun that ripened you from earth
Pushing south winds

Through lands without belief till this pretty birth
The faithful finds:
Fanatic doves, believing wrens and orioles
Devoted redwinged blackbirds with their calls,
Archilochus alexandri,
Melospiza georgiana,
All surround you with arched cries of Love's triumphals.

Your mind is a nest of all young things, all children
Come to this meadow forest edge;
Put her together
From this squirrel corn dogtooth young sedge
And all this weather
Of the white bloodroots to be her skin
The wake robin to be her shin
Her thighs pockets
Of white violets
Her breasts the gleaming soft pearly everlasting.

For her limbs are the rivers of Eden;
Her face unlocks
The brown merry bear from his den,
From his box
The butterfly and her body is a bethlehem
Humming
With cherubim
And her mind is a cloud of all young things, all children.

The prize to this one goes cried eagerly some
And others cried that to Raymond it must come,
So that Duncan Goose turned to the plantain leaf
And chopped the prize in half with beak-thrust brief.

The Alphabet

Where are the fields of dew?
I cannot keep them.
They quip and pun
The rising sun
Who plucks them out of view:
But lay down fire-veined jasper!

For out of my cloudy head
Come Ay Ee I Oh and U,
Five thunders shouted;
Drive in sardonyx!

And Ull Mm Nn Rr and hisSsings
Proclaim huge wings;
Pour in sea blue sapphires!

Through my bristling hair
Blows Wuh and Yuh
Puh, Buh, Phuh and Vuh,
The humorous air:
Lift up skies of chalcedony!

Huh, Cuh, Guh and Chuh
Grunt like pigs in my acorn mind:
Arrange these emeralds in a meadow!

Come down Tuh, Duh and Thuh!
Consonantly rain
On the windowpane
Of the shrunken house of the heart;
Lift up blood red sardius!

Lift up golden chrysolite!
Juh, Quuh, Zuh and X
Scribble heavens with light,
Steeples take fright.

In my mouth like bread
Stands the shape of this glory;
Consonants and vowels
Repeat the story:
And sea-green beryl is carried up!

The candle tongue in my dark mouth
Is anguished with its sloth
And stung with self-scoff
As my eyes behold this treasure.
Let them bring up topaz now!

Dazzling chrysoprase!
Dewdrops tempt dark wick to sparkle.
Growl Spark! you whelp and cur,
Leap out of tongue kennel
And candle sepulchre.

I faint in the hyacinthine quarries!
My words pursue
Through the forest of time
The fading antlers of this dew.

A B C D E F G H I J K L M
Take captive the sun
Slay the dew quarry
Adam's Eve is morning rib
Bride and bridegroom marry
Still coffin is rocking crib
Tower and well are one
The stone is the wind, the wind is the stone
New Jerusalem
N O P Q R S T U V W X Y Z!

First Letter

TO THE AVON RIVER ABOVE STRATFORD, CANADA

What did the Indians call you?
For you do not flow
With English accents.
I hardly know
What I should call you
      Because before
I drank coffee or tea
      I drank you
      With my cupped hands
And you did not taste English to me
      And you do not sound
      Like Avon
      Or swans & bards
But rather like the sad wild fowl
      In prints drawn
      By Audubon
And like dear bad poets
      Who wrote
      Early in Canada
And never were of note.
You are the first river
      I crossed
And like the first whirlwind
      The first rainbow
      First snow, first
      Falling star I saw,
You, for other rivers are my law.
      These other rivers:
      The Red & the Thames
      Are never so sweet
To skate upon, swim in
      Or for baptism of sin.
      Silver and light
The sentence of your voice,

With a soprano
Continuous cry you shall
   Always flow
   Through my heart.
The rain and the snow of my mind
Shall supply the spring of that river
   Forever.
Though not your name
Your coat of arms I know
   And motto:
A shield of reeds and cresses
   Sedges, crayfishes
The hermaphroditic leech
Minnows, muskrats and farmers' geese
And printed above this shield
One of my earliest wishes
"To flow like you."

The Sundogs

I saw the sundogs barking
On either side of the Sun
And he was making his usual will
And last testament
In a glorious vestment.
And the sundogs cried,
"Bow wow!
We'll make a ring
Around the moon
And children, seeing it, will say:
Up there they play Farmer in the Dell
And the moon like the cheese stands still.
Bow wow!
We shall drown the crickets,
Set the killdeer birds crying,
Send shingles flying,
And pick all the apples
Ripe or not.

Our barking shall overturn
Hencoops and rabbit-hutches,
Shall topple over privies
With people inside them,
And burn with invisible,
Oh, very invisible!
Flames
In each frightened tree.
Whole branches we'll bite off
And for the housewife's sloth
In not taking them in
We'll drag her sheets and pillow cases
Off the fence
And dress up in them
And wear them thin.
And people will say
Both in the country
And in the town
It falls in pails
Of iron nails.
We'll blow the curses
Right back into the farmer's mouths
As they curse our industry
And shake their fists,
For we will press the oats
Close to the ground,
Lodge the barley,
And rip open the wheat stooks.
We shall make great faces
Of dampness appear on ceilings
And blow down chimneys
Till the fire's lame.
With the noise of a thousand typewriters
We shall gallop over the roofs of town.
We are the Sun's animals.
We stand by him in the West
And ready to obey
His most auburn wish
For Rain, Wind and Storm.''

ROBERT KROETSCH

b. 1927

Pumpkin: A Love Poem

Inside the pumpkin   I feel much better
I feel   loyalty to my pioneering
ancestors   I have entered

new territory   I feel a bit
sticky, yes, cramped   but I feel
much better   trying to smile

I take out my knife   I cut
one triangular   hole
into the pale flesh   of my new

head   and then, gently
the tip of the knife   to my left
eyeball,   gently I twist

lift the old eye   to its new vision
of pea vines   snared in wire
and lettuce   gone to towering seed

and then   oh, what the hell
the second eye   no, not
quite yet   as blind as

love, I cut the new nose   flared
to demonstrate my   innate
ferocity   I slice off

my nose   and let it
sniff its way   into the scent of
staked tomatoes   and drying dill

I cut the new mouth   the place that
must be   toothed and jagged
the slit   that will

sneer   and then, about to
slice out   the old
I feel   on my pressing groin

the new mouth   on my cradled
like the seeds that   cradle
the new mouth   pressing

and then   squirming uneasily
inside the pumpkin   I am able
just barely   able to unzip

and she, outside   walking
in her garden   sees
my magnificent   unfallen

nature   my recovered ancestry
of borders   bravely crossed
and husbandry   triumphant

What are you doing   in my
pumpkin   she says, and I
muffled   sticky   humped

(I feel much better)   go
away, I shout   can't you see
at last   can't you see

leave me alone   (thrusting
with all my innate   ferocity)
at last, at last   can't you see
I'm fucking the whole world.

Winter Birds

The winter birds   outside my window
feed in the sumac   hide in the green
juniper   eat and sleep

and in their season   lust
have their winter   and lust
again in season   while I

waiting for you to answer the phone
eat pretzels   drink gin
unseasoned   open the door

(even the birds avoid me   fly
into the neighbor's maple)   feeling
a new desire   to know, to share

I go down the back steps   (avoiding
the ice, of course)   I climb up into
the sumac   clinging

I perch   (listening for the phone)
the birds return   I am pleased
they trust my   nest-like

head   my long bare arms
they speak   syllables only
and I   I am very still

I open my mouth   slowly
I try a grunt   a squawk
no answer   I try a friendly trill

no answer   I don't even know
their names   not owls
not jays   not magpies

birds, I ask them   how, how
no answer   birds, I ask them
what degree of zero   what

absolute cold   will make me
harder than   no answer
what length of night will satisfy

what iron winter will it take
to free   what polar
year   what ice cap

no answer   the birds
crowd against me   oh mother
mother, mother   is death

no answer   they peck at my
shoes, at my knees   they find
moth eggs   in my thighs

I am pleased   they find
winter buds   on my fingers
life isn't so bad   I assure them

life isn't so bad   they peck the
seeds from my tongue   they sleep
in my warm crotch   spring

will get here   I assure them
life isn't so bad   don't worry
spring will get here   don't worry

Elegy for Wong Toy

Charlie   you are dead now
but I dare to speak because
in China the living speak
to their kindred   dead.
And you are one of my fathers.

Your iron bachelorhood perplexed
our horny youth: we were born
to the snow of a prairie town
to the empty streets of our
longing.   You built a railway
                              to get there.

You were your own enduring   winter.
You were your abacus, your Chinaman's
eyes.   You were the long reach up
to the top of that bright showcase
where   for a few pennies
we bought a whole childhood.

Only a Christmas calendar
told us your name:
Wong Toy, prop., Canada Cafe:
above the thin pad of months,
under the almost naked girl
in the white leather boots
who was never allowed to undress
in the rows of God-filled houses

which you were never
invited to enter.

Charlie, I knew my first touch
of Ellen Kiefer's young breasts
in the second booth from the back
                              in your cafe.

It was the night of a hockey game.
You were out in the kitchen
making sandwiches and coffee.

You were your own enduring
winter.   You were our spring
and we   like meadowlarks
hearing the sun   boom
under the flat horizon
cracked the still dawn alive
with one ferocious   song.

So Charlie   this is a thank you
poem.   You are twenty years
dead.   I hope they buried you
sitting upright in your grave
the way you sat   pot-bellied
behind your jawbreakers
and your licorice plugs,
behind your tins of Ogden's fine cut,
your treasury of cigars,

and the heart-shaped box of chocolates
that no one ever took home.

F. P. Grove: The Finding

1.

Dreaming the well-born   hobo of yourself
against the bourgeois father   dreaming Europe
if only to find   a place to be from

the hobo tragedian   pitching bundles
riding a freight   to the impossible city
the fallen archangel   of Brandon or Winnipeg

in all your harvesting   real
or imagined   did you really find
four aged stallions   neigh

in your cold undertaking   on those trails north
in all the (dreamed) nights   in stooks
in haystacks   dreaming the purified dreamer

who lured you   to a new man (back
to the fatal earth)   inventing (beyond
America)   a new world   did you find

did you dream   the French priest who hauled you
out of your *fleurs du mal*   and headlong
into a hundred drafts   real

or imagined   of the sought form
(there are no models)   and always
(there are only models)   alone

  2.

alone in the cutter   in the blizzard
two horses   hauling you into the snow
that buries the road   burying the forest

the layered mind   exfoliating
back to the barren sea   (Greek to us,
Grove)   back to the blank sun

and musing snow to yourself   new
to the old rite of burial   the snow
lifting the taught man   into the coyote self

the silence of sight   "as if I were not myself
who yet am I"   riding the drifted snow
to your own plummeting   alone and alone

the *wirklichkeit*   of the word itself
the name under the name   the sought
and calamitous edge   of the white earth

the horses   pawing the empty fall
the hot breath on the zero day   the man
seeing the new man so vainly   alone

we say with your waiting wife   (but she
was the world   before you invented it
old liar)   "You had a hard trip?"

Stone Hammer Poem   *— Artifact of Indians.*

1.

This stone
become a hammer
of stone, this maul

is the colour
of bone (no, *← under Purdy's tuition —*
bone is the colour   *very honest. Also*
of this stone maul).   *makes reader*
    aware of time

The rawhide loops   *indicates*
are gone, the   *lastingness of*
hand is gone, the   *natural*
buffalo's skull   *Things*
is gone;

the stone is
shaped like the skull
of a child.   *— Simile*

2.

This paperweight on my desk

where I begin
this poem   was

found in a wheatfield
lost (this hammer,
this poem).

Cut to a function,
this stone was
(the hand is   gone—

*Jumbled Thoughts
gives sense of
immediacy*

3.

Grey, two-headed,
the pemmican maul

fell from the travois or
a boy playing   lost it in
the prairie wool or
a squaw   left it in
the brain of a buffalo or

It is a million
years older than
the hand that
chipped stone or
raised slough
water (or blood) or   *- left hanging*

4.

This stone maul
was found.

n the field
ny grandfather
hought
vas his

ny father
hought was his

[handwritten: Play on words. "old thoughts" or what his grandfather actually thought]

5.

t is a stone
ld as the last
Ice Age, the
retreating / the
recreating ice,
the retreating
buffalo, the
retreating Indians

(the saskatoons bloom
white (infrequently
the chokecherries the
highbush cranberries the
pincherries bloom
white along the barbed
wire fence (the
pemmican   winter

6.

This stone maul
stopped a plow
long enough for one
Gott im Himmel.

[handwritten: Nature is more powerful that anything]

The Blackfoot (the   → *[handwritten: Indian theme]*
Cree?) not

finding the maul
cursed.

?did he curse
?did he try to
go back
?what happened
I have to/ I want
to know (not know)
?WHAT HAPPENED

[handwritten marginalia: - ? go back to past to find answers.]

7.

The poem
is the stone
chipped and hammered
until it is shaped
like the stone
hammer, the maul.

8.

Now the field is
mine because
I gave it
(for a price)

to a young man
(with a growing son)
who did not

notice that the land
did not belong
to the Indian who
gave it to the Queen
(for a price) who
gave it to the CPR
(for a price) which
gave it to my grandfather
(for a price) who
gave it to my father
(50 bucks an acre

Gott.im Himmel I cut
down all the trees I
picked up all the stones) who

gave it to his son
(who sold it)

9.

This won't
surprise you.

My grandfather
lost the stone maul.

10.

My father (retired)
grew raspberries.
He dug in his potato patch.
He drank one glass of wine
each morning.
He was lonesome
for death.

He was lonesome for the
hot wind on his face, the smell
of horses, the distant
hum of a threshing machine,
the oilcan he carried, the weight
of a crescent wrench in his hind pocket.

He was lonesome for his absent
son and his daughters,
for his wife, for his own
brothers and sisters and
his own mother and father.

He found the stone maul
on a rockpile in the
north-west corner of what
he thought of
as his wheatfield.

He kept it (the
stone maul) on the railing
of the back porch in
a raspberry basket.

11.

I keep it
on my desk
(the stone).

Sometimes I use it
in the (hot) wind
(to hold down paper)

smelling a little of cut
grass or maybe even of
ripening wheat or of
buffalo blood hot
in the dying sun.

Sometimes I write
my poems for that

stone hammer.

to the dark side of Canada.

Mile Zero: being some account of a journey through western Canada in the dead of six nights

1.

I looked at the dust
on the police car hood.
I looked around the horizon.
(Insert here passage on
nature—
    try: The sun was blight
          enough for the wild rose.
          A musky flavour on the milk
          foretold the cracked earth . . .
    try: One crow foresaw my fright,
          leaned out of the scalding
          air, and ate a grasshopper's
          warning . . .
    try: A whirlwind of gulls
          burned the black field white,
          burned white the dark ploughman
          and the coming night . . .)

I AM A SIMPLE POET
I wrote in the dust
on the police car hood.

[handwritten annotations in margins:]

night / white
fright
blight

Published w/ own draft notes makes it funnier

3 stanza lyric w/ Rhyme

"I will not be old fashioned poetry - it is not appropriate write"

Kroetsch - intellectual jokes - very funny as poetry

Parisian Wit / Raunchy AB comedy

for AB anyway

2.

Where did the virgin come from
on my second night west?
    Let me, prosaically, parenthetically, remark
    upon what I observed: the lady in question took
    from the left (or was it right?) pocket of her
    coffee-stained apron a small square pad of lined
    sheets of paper. She bit the wood back from
    the lead of a stub of pencil. And she wrote,
    without once stopping to think, the loveliest
    goddamned (I had gauged her breasts when she
    wiped the table) poem that Christ ever read.
She had a clean mind.

3.

On the third night west
a mountain stopped us.
The mountains were lined up
to dance. I raised my baton:
rooted in earth, the lightning
rod of the roof of the barn,
on my soul's body. A crow
flew over the moon. I raised
my baton, a moon, a mountain.
(Verily, I insist: I did
not raise the purple crow.)
The crow flew over the mountain.

4.

Order, gentlemen. Order
(her breasts were paradigms)
is the ultimate
mountain. I raised my baton.

penis erection

5.

The bindertwine of place—
The mansource of the man—
The natural odour of stinkweed—
The ache at the root of
                    the spinal thrust—
(Despair is   not writing the poem,
say what you will about despair.)

6.

What I took to be an eagle
turned out to be a gull.
We glimpsed the sea.
The road ended
but it did not end:
the crying gulls turned
on the moon. The moon
was in the sea.
Despair that had sought the moon's
meaning found now the moon.
(Mile Zero is everywhere.)
the roar of the sea was the sea's roar.

*unfulfilled dreams?
loss of expectations?
innocence lost?*

The Silent Poet Sees Red

and green too, on occasion, granted

but I wouldn't slander a friend for the world, cross
      my heart

and spit to die

but he shuts off his inboard motor, he sprawls on the
      deck of his cottage, nursing a beer, he forgets to
      shave for a week

and he thinks he's a sailor, Earache the Red; it was he
      who discovered dry land

but sit yourself down, he promises, life is short

and while you're up, crack us a couple of cold ones,
      poet

but I hardly have time, he talks too much; he is Professor
      of Nowhere at some place or other; puck, he says,
      waving a stick

and he skates his way through class, defying entropy,
      slamming the puck under the chairs of his sleeping
      students

but women are fooled by his library, ha; he's all show;
      may he rupture himself, clipping his toenails

and while I'm on the subject, his wife has four arms,
      she holds him together, blind as love

but remember, the pupil is black, we see with darkness
      only

and I watch for a light in the west, occidents will
      happen, ho

but sunrise comes at noon to her bed

and what do we have for lunch, breakfast; Silent Poet,
      she tells me, you are the great keeper, the wellspring
      of was, the guardian of ought

but that's your loss, not mine

and soft as blue she whispers a pip into her palm; west
      is a color of the wind

PHYLLIS WEBB

b. 1927

Breaking

Give us wholeness, for we are broken.
But who are we asking, and why do we ask?
Destructive element heaves close to home,
our years of work broken against a breakwater.

Shattered gods, self-iconoclasts,
it is with Lazarus unattended we belong
(the fall of the sparrow is unbroken song).
The crucifix has clattered to the gound,
the living Christ has spent a year in Paris,
travelled on the Métro, fallen in the Seine.
We would not raise our silly gods again.
Stigmata sting, they suddenly appear
on every blessed person everywhere.
If there is agitation there is cause.

Ophelia, Hamlet, Othello, Lear,
Kit Smart, William Blake, John Clare,
Van Gogh, Henry IV of Pirandello,
Gerard de Nerval, Antonin Artaud
bear a crown of darkness.
It is better so.

Responsible now each to his own attack,
we are bequeathed their ethos and our deatl
Greek marble white and whiter grows
breaking into history of a west.
If we could stand so virtuously white
crumbling in the terrible Grecian light.

There is a justice in destruction.
It isn't 'isn't fair'.
A madhouse is designed for the insane,
a hospital for wounds that will re-open;
a war is architecture for aggression,
and Christ's stigmata body-minted token.
What are we whole or beautiful or good for
but to be absolutely broken?

Marvell's Garden

Marvell's garden, that place of solitude,
is not where I'd choose to live
yet is the fixed sundial
that turns me round
unwillingly
in a hot glade
as closer, closer I come to contradiction
to the shade green within the green shade.

The garden where Marvell scorned love's solicitude—
that dream—and played instead an arcane solitaire,
shuffling his thoughts like shadowy chance
across the shrubs of ecstasy,
and cast the myths away to flowering hours
as yes, his mind, that sea, caught at green
thoughts shadowing a green infinity.

And yet Marvell's garden was not Plato's
garden—and yet—he did care more for the form
of things than for the thing itself—
ideas and visions,
resemblances and echoes,
things seeming and being
not quite what they were.

That was his garden, a kind of attitude
struck out of an earth too carefully attended,
wanting to be left alone.
And I don't blame him for that.
God knows, too many fences fence us out
and his garden closed in on Paradise.

On Paradise! When I think of his hymning
Puritans in the Bermudas, the bright oranges
lighting up that night! When I recall
his rustling tinsel hopes
beneath the cold decree of steel,
Oh, I have wept for some new convulsion
to tear together this world and his.

But then I saw his luminous plumèd Wings
prepared for flight,
and then I heard him singing glory
in a green tree,
and then I caught the vest he'd laid aside
all blest with fire.

And I have gone walking slowly in
his garden of necessity
leaving brothers, lovers, Christ
outside my walls
where they have wept without
and I within.

The Shape of Prayer

The shape of prayer
is like the shape of the small
beach stone, rounded smooth, but individual
in its despair,
skimmed on the water it skips to drown
down with its sunken fellows, down
in despair.

The shape of prayer is that—
curved and going nowhere, to fall
in pure abstraction saying everything
and saying nothing at all.

Poetics Against the Angel of Death

I am sorry to speak of death again
(some say I'll have a long life)
but last night Wordsworth's 'Prelude'
suddenly made sense—I mean the measure,
the elevated tone, the attitude
of private Man speaking to public men.
Last night I thought I would not wake again
but now with this June morning I run ragged to elude
The Great Iambic Pentameter
who is the Hound of Heaven in our stress
because I want to die
writing Haiku
or, better,
long lines, clean and syllabic as knotted bamboo. Yes!

Eschatology of Spring

Death, Judgement, Heaven, Hell,
and Spring. The Five Last Things,
the least of which I am, being in
the azaleas and dog-toothed violets
of the South of Canada. Do not tell me
this is a cold country. I am also in
the camelias and camas of early, of
abrupt birth.
We are shooting up for the bloody
judgement of the six o'clock news.
Quick, cut us out from the deadlines
of rotting newspapers, quick, for the

tiny skeletons and bulbs will tell you
how death grows and grows in Chile and
Chad. Quick, for the small bones pinch
me and insects divulge occult excrement
in the service of my hyacinth, my trailing
begonia. And if you catch me resting
beside the stream, sighing against
the headlines of this pastoral, take
up your gun, the flowers blossoming
from its barrel, and join this grief, this
grief: that there are lambs, elegant black-
footed lambs in this island's eschatology,
Beloved.

A Question of Questions

I.

question
query
hook
        of the soul
        a question of
questions

                    why/how
                        oh God
                    has it come to this

hook
sickle
scythe
   to cut us down this
mark?
    who—how many years
    to shape the mind to make
    its turn toward this?

the where / when of the type
the proper fall of lead
in the printer's font?
and who are you in this
school
room
torture chamber
whose are you?
and what of your
trials and errors?
the judge
in his echo chamber
cannot know
and nor can you
you cannot answer

II.

Succulent lobe of the ear
droplet of flesh
depending from the not
quite crescent you are
allowed to hear with.
Does it know what I say?
Can it imagine my sentence?
I bring my head near.
I whisper.
I flicker my tongue in tricks.
I taste the stare of its mischief.
I riddle my enterprise.
I shut my mouth and open my eyes.
Suddenly I do not love
that ornament, that place.
Turn your head.
I want to see your face.

III.

The hello of your mouth is what I want
the smile of your crooked pearlies.
Whatever *is* rustles existence out of some
mouth, stuffs essence into some other.
                    Fancy talk
                        in the continuum
                            of my wanting
                        a word / the word / the
                    occult withdrawn-ness of it
                        I endure that
                                            or suffer busy-
                        bodies' oneway chatter
                            fools of time ungladly.
Hello / hello is as equal as we'll come
                                    my love
                        my question
                    my answer
                        smiles on one side,
ugly, or other of
                        power and seduction.
Scene / Riviera
        villa's shutters clap and boo Monsieur
                        Sun, Mistral, Peeping
        Tom who want my names
                    your many occupations.
Let's shutter ourselves in sleep.
        (Where did your mouth go?
                    why didn't you say hello?)
Dark, take their inquisition.
        Thinking, at best,
                    is dreaming
                        chase and quarry
        hounds at bay
                    horses and riding masters

the decay of all that
        into morning
                    where nothing is
        not over, never done with
                        once and for all
                                All eyes!
I remember my dream of last night's raiding cops
who judged my love-making for a contest.
The night before you stunned a Minister
of Justice, who must have passed the word.
I can't answer for nuance and spectrum.
The case doesn't hold.
Try wearing a ring.
        try going for aquamarine and losing.
Or. Topaz. Opal. Ultras. Primes.
        The pigments of Bosch
                        dismay the drift of your
                                nightmare
my waves of Dufy.
        Sleep on my love, my lovely.
I'll hum the blues. I'll monologue
        Our little lives . . .
                    Our voluptuous questing . . .

    IV.

Extracted toenails.
I have nothing to say.

Burns on the breasts.
I have nothing to say.

Electric shock.
I have nothing to say.

Beatings.
I have nothing to say.

Refinements of an old skill.
Make the inner outer.

I am what I am.
All one.

Done. Take it away.

V. *(for R.D.L.)*

The error lies in
the state of desire
in wanting the answers
wanting the red-crested
woodpecker to pose
among red berries
of the ash tree
wanting its names
its habitations
the instinct
of its ways for
my head-travelling
wanting its colours
its red, white, its black
pressed behind my eyes
a triptych
three-fold
and over
and wanting the bird
to be still and
wanting it moving
whiteflash of underwings
dazzling all questions
out of me, amazement
and outbreathing
become a form
of my knowing,

I move and it moves
into a cedar tree.
I walk and I walk.

My deceiving angel's
in-shadow joins me
paces my steps and threatens
to take my head
between its hands.
I keep walking.
Trying to think.
Here on the island
there is time
on the Isabella
Point Road.
We pass a dead
deer on the beach.
Bloated. It stinks.
The angel insists, 'Keep
walking. It has all the time
in the world. Is sufficient.
Is alone. Keep walking,'
it says and flies off
with my head.

What's left of me
remembers a funny song
also a headless
man on rockface
painted in red
by Indian finger spirits.

The red-crested woodpecker swoops down
and sits on my trunk. Posing.
Dryocopus pileatus. 'Spectacular, black,
Crow-sized woodpecker with a red *crest*,
great size, sweeping wingbeats, flashing
white underwing.' Pileated woodpecker.
Posing. Many questions.
'The diggings, large *oval* or *oblong* holes,
indicate its presence.'

Zen Master.

D. G. JONES

b. 1929

Boy in the Lamont Poetry Room, Harvard

His mouth babbling under the earphones,
Rocked by a rhetoric I cannot hear—

Who should be surprised if, suddenly,
He flew into air, disappeared

In one feathered burst, Thoth,
Wild with declamation—if he left

Us standing, dumb, more or less stable,
Like so many cows, Chagall's, in a shaken world?

Devil's Paint Brush

After the rain
They are a rust upon the field,

They are suns
Burning in a spider's space,

They are
Nipples by Matisse—One

White daisy
Is a virgin or a saint,
A vestal in a host of flames.

Musk is their smell,
Like sunlight on a girl's face.

Portrait of Anne Hébert

The sunlight, here and there,
Touches a table

And a draught at the window
Announces your presence,

You take your place in the room
Without fuss,

Your delicate bones,
Your frock,
Have the grace of disinterested passion.

Words are arrayed
Like surgical instruments
Neatly in trays.

Deftly, you make an incision
Probing
The obscure disease.

Your sensibility
Has the sure fingers of the blind:

Each decision
Cuts like a scalpel
Through tangled emotion.

You define
The morbid tissue, laying it bare

Like a tatter of lace
Dark
On the paper.

I Thought There Were Limits

I thought there were limits, Newtonian
Laws of emotion —

I thought there were limits to this falling away,
This emptiness. I was wrong.

The apples, falling, never hit the ground.

So much for grass, and animals —
Nothing remains,
No sure foundation on the rock. The cat

Drifts, or simply dissolves.

L'homme moyen sensuel
Had better look out: complete
Deprivation brings

Dreams, hallucinations which reveal
The sound and fury of machines
Working on nothing — which explains

God's creation: *ex nihilo fecit.*

Wrong again. I now suspect
The limit is the sea itself,
The limitless.

So, neither swim nor float. Relax.
The void is not so bleak.

Conclude: desire is but an ache,
An absence. It creates
A dream of limits

And it grows in gravity as that takes shape.

Washed Up

The rock
rising from water,

cedars
twisting from rock,

clouds
and a single birch —

Nausicaa
playing in the wind.

Untitled Poem

From sex, this sea, we have emerged
into a quiet room
our bodies bare

We have been washed by tides
the glacial waters welling up
to shudder and subside, the broad streams

wandering to the pole

The climate of the flesh
is temperate here
though we look out on a winter world

We are the islanders
between two seasons, and a garden where
we are the botanists

of our own flowers. And yet

I am led into the winter air
by certain nameless twigs, as bare
as we are. I would find

them also in our mouths

Untitled Poem

I annihilate the purple finch
in the apple tree

it is a winter dawn

it is 'La Guerre' Henri Rousseau
saw charging through the shattered space
of the Second Empire

it is a faint
raspberry
in the silent cosmos

c'est une tache
sur la page blanche

un cauchemar en rose

c'est le Québec
libre

a bird

c'est ça
un oiseau dans un pommier

it may fly off
but it won't go away

I neglected to mention the snow

JAY MACPHERSON

b. 1931

The Anagogic Man

Noah walks with head bent down;
For between his nape and crown
He carries, balancing with care,
A golden bubble round and rare.

Its gently shimmering sides surround
All us and our worlds, and bound
Art and life, and wit and sense,
Innocence and experience.

Forbear to startle him, lest some
Poor soul to its destruction come,
Slipped out of mind and past recall
As if it never was at all.

O you that pass, if still he seems
One absent-minded or in dreams,
Consider that your senses keep
A death far deeper than his sleep.

Angel, declare: what sways when Noah nods?
The sun, the stars, the figures of the gods.

The Boatman

You might suppose it easy
For a maker not too lazy
To convert the gentle reader to an Ark:

But it takes a willing pupil
To admit both gnat and camel
—Quite an eyeful, all the crew that must embark.

After me when comes the deluge
And you're looking round for refuge
From God's anger pouring down in gush and spout,
Then you take the tender creature
—You remember, that's the reader —
And you pull him through his navel inside out.

That's to get his beasts outside him,
For they've got to come aboard him,
As the best directions have it, two by two.
When you've taken all their tickets
And you've marched them through his sockets,
Let the tempest bust Creation: heed not you.

For you're riding high and mighty
In a gale that's pushing ninety
With a solid bottom under you —that's his.
Fellow flesh affords a rampart,
And you've got along for comfort
All the world there ever shall be, was, and is.

The Fisherman

The world was first a private park
Until the angel, after dark,
Scattered afar to wests and easts
The lovers and the friendly beasts.

And later still a home-made boat
Contained Creation set afloat,
No rift nor leak that might betray
The creatures to a hostile day.

But now beside the midnight lake
One single fisher sits awake
And casts and fights and hauls to land
A myriad forms upon the sand.

Old Adam on the naming-day
Blessed each and let it slip away:
The fisher of the fallen mind
Sees no occasion to be kind,

But on his catch proceeds to sup;
Then bends, and at one slurp sucks up
The lake and all that therein is
To slake that hungry gut of his,

Then whistling makes for home and bed
As the last morning breaks in red;
But God the Lord with patient grin
Lets down his hook and hoicks him in.

Hecate Trivia

Here in a land of faultless four-leaved clovers,
Learning from books how, back before our windows,
Mirrors, your dusty forks were where uncanny
    Worlds faced each other,

We, where our fathers banished wolf and Indian,
Vainly regret their vanished sense and vigour:
Now in our cities take a last, last stand with
    Rat and with cockroach.

Goddess of crossways, three-faced, was it you my
Muse all this while? you are the last who hallows
Contents of pockets, broken dolls, dead puppies:
    Queen, garbage-eater.

In That Cellar

Where I laid my   murdered brother,
Where I laid my   angry mother,
Where I laid my   luckless sister,
     In that cellar
They lie, they lie, they lie.

Stitched with wires and   gashed with axes,
Bound with chains and   mummy-swaddled,
Eyes pricked out and   spines unthreaded,
     In that cellar
They wait, they wait, they wait.

There I lie, to   them committed,
Theirs my hope, and   theirs my patience,
Till the judgement,   till light finds us,
     In that cellar
Is all, is all, is all.

What Falada Said

All I have left from home—the horse that brought me,
Dead, flayed, its head hung up, its power of speaking
Left, like an echo—gives its daily message
     In the dark entry:

'Daughter, betrayed and drudging here in exile,
Those who let these things happen were—believe me—
Foreigners, strangers, none of those who loved you:
     Not your true mother.

She if she knew would send someone to fetch you,
Carry you home, restore the past, again her
Child, joy from pain: at least, if she could know it
     She would be sorry.'

So on my nursery floor my dolls consoled me.
No: there are four, not two: a constellation
Turning: maimed child, barbed mother—torn, rent open
     Womb, bladed baby.

ALDEN NOWLAN

b. 1933

Looking For Nancy

Looking for Nancy
      everywhere, I've stopped
girls in trenchcoats
and blue dresses,
      said
Nancy I've looked
      all over
         hell for you,
Nancy I've been afraid
I'd die before I found you.

      But there's always
      been some mistake:

a broken streetlight,
too much rum
      or even
my wanting too much
for it to be her.

The Bull Moose

Down from the purple mist of trees on the mountain,
lurching through forests of white spruce and cedar,
stumbling through tamarack swamps,
came the bull moose
to be stopped at last by a pole-fenced pasture.

Too tired to turn or, perhaps, aware
there was no place left to go, he stood with the cattle.
They, scenting the musk of death, seeing his great head
like the ritual mask of a blood god, moved to the other end
of the field and waited.

The neighbours heard of it, and by afternoon
cars lined the road. The children teased him
with alder switches and he gazed at them
like an old tolerant collie. The women asked
if he could have escaped from a Fair.

The oldest man in the parish remembered seeing
a gelded moose yoked with an ox for plowing.
The young men snickered and tried to pour beer
down his throat, while their girl friends
took their pictures.

And the bull moose let them stroke his tick-ravaged flanks,
let them pry open his jaws with bottles, let a giggling girl
plant a little purple cap
of thistles on his head.

When the wardens came, everyone agreed it was a shame
to shoot anything so shaggy and cuddlesome.
He looked like the kind of pet
women put to bed with their sons.

So they held their fire. But just as the sun dropped
        in the river
the bull moose gathered his strength
like a scaffolded king, straightened and lifted his horns
so that even the wardens backed away as they raised
        their rifles.
When he roared, people ran to their cars. All the young men
leaned on their automobile horns as he toppled.

The Mysterious Naked Man

A mysterious naked man has been reported
on Cranston Avenue. The police are performing
the usual ceremonies with coloured lights and sirens.
Almost everyone is outdoors and strangers are conversing
        excitedly
as they do during disasters when their involvement is
        peripheral.
"What did he look like?" the lieutenant is asking.
"I don't know," says the witness. "He was naked."
There is talk of dogs—this is no ordinary case
of indecent exposure, the man has been seen
a dozen times since the milkman spotted him and now
the sky is turning purple and voices
carry a long way and the children
have gone a little crazy as they often do at dusk
and cars are arriving
from other sections of the city.
And the mysterious naked man
is kneeling behind a garbage can or lying on his belly
in somebody's garden
or maybe even hiding in the branches of a tree,
where the wind from the harbour
whips at his naked body,
and by now he's probably done
whatever it was he wanted to do
and wishes he could go to sleep
or die
or take to the air like Superman.

The Execution

On the night of the execution
a man at the door
mistook me for the coroner.
"Press," I said.

But he didn't understand. He led me
into the wrong room
where the sheriff greeted me:
"You're late, Padre."

"You're wrong," I told him. "I'm Press."
"Yes, of course, Reverend Press."
We went down a stairway.

"Ah, Mr. Ellis," said the Deputy.
"Press!" I shouted. But he shoved me
through a black curtain.
The lights were so bright
I couldn't see the faces
of the men sitting
opposite. But, thank God, I thought
they can see me!

"Look!" I cried. "Look at my face!
Doesn't anybody know me?"

Then a hood covered my head.
"Don't make it harder for us," the hangman whispered.

The broadcaster's poem

I used to broadcast at night
alone in a radio station
but I was never good at it,
partly because my voice wasn't right
but mostly because my peculiar
metaphysical stupidity
made it impossible
for me to keep believing
there was somebody listening
when it seemed I was talking
only to myself in a room no bigger
than an ordinary bathroom.
I could believe it for a while
and then I'd get somewhat
the same feeling as when you
start to suspect you're the victim
of a practical joke.
                              So one part of me
was afraid another part
might blurt out something
about myself so terrible
that even I had never until
that moment suspected it.
                              This was like the fear
of bridges and other
high places: Will I take off my glasses
and throw them
into the water, although I'm
half-blind without them?
Will I sneak up behind
myself and push?
                              Another thing:
as a reporter
I covered an accident in which a train
ran into a car, killing
three young men, one of whom
was beheaded. The bodies looked

oneless, as such bodies do.
More like mounds of rags.
And inside the wreckage
where nobody could get at it
the car radio
was still playing.

        I thought about places
the disc jockey's voice goes
and the things that happen there
and of how impossible it would be for him
to continue if he really knew.

The Unhappy People

Professor, may I introduce you
to two of the Unhappy People, whom you've described
as inhabiting a cultural vacuum
somewhere between the swamps of Frustration
and the salt sea of Despair.
May I present my wife's cousins, Corey and Brent.
You will note immediately that their teeth are translucent,
the colour of reconstituted powdered milk,
which can be attributed to hereditary malnutrition,
as their lack of ear-lobes can be ascribed to inbreeding.
You are free to make notes, if you wish.
At worst, they'll merely laugh at you.

Professor, I must ask you to forgive
the mandolin, the five-string banjo, the guitar, the fiddle
and the jew's-harp. I must ask you to bear with
Brent when he dances—he prefers it to walking to
the refrigerator for another beer—and Corey when he
    scratches
his groin in symbolic tribute to the girl in the yellow
    bathing suit
playing with a frisbee on the grass across the street.
I know it's distracting when, for no apparent reason,
they break into song. I can understand your not laughing

with them when they talk about driving
four-year-old cars at one hundred and ten
miles per hour down dirt roads with the police behind them,
of overturning and wondering drunkenly how to shut off
the headlights, until logic triumphed and they kicked
    them out.
I beg you not to be disturbed when they whoop
at the tops of their voices—it's in their blood,
I'm afraid, their way of declaring an instantaneous holiday
and, besides, Brent got out of jail this morning
or, as he puts it, got back from his annual vacation,
having been locked up this time because he didn't
know his own strength, he says, and when he was refused
    service
at the liquor store, being drunk, forgot he was carrying
nothing under his left arm to offset the force of his right
pushing open the door on his way out and so, purely by
    accident,
drove his fist through the glass:
it could have happened to anybody, Your Honour,
he told the Court. You must excuse Corey, Professor,
like every member of his family he walks in and out
of rooms without thinking it necessary to offer
any explanation. When they arrive at my house
or any other, they open the door, come in, sit down
and, perhaps, switch on the radio. They'd expect you to do
    the same.
If you go to the window, Professor, you'll see
that he's talking with the girl in the yellow bathing suit
and already has her laughing. "Once you got them
    laughing,
you're as good as in bed with them," Brent says.
    In celebration
he jumps up again and dances. They've brought venison
and wild rice and a half-dozen jars of their mother's
homemade preserves and pickles, fresh loaves of her bread
two double cases of beer and a forty-ounce bottle
of dark rum, having shut down the cannery
where Corey works in honour of Brent's homecoming.

"I said to hell with 'er, let's tie 'er up."
and with unanimous approval of his fellows,
conveyed without a word, he tied her up well
by making certain delicate adjustments to the machinery
when the bosses weren't watching. His laughter and his
      brother's
laughter and the laughter of the girl in the yellow bathing
      suit
mingle and rise like water from a garden hose, spraying the
      windows
from inside and out. The passersby turn
and smile, a neighbour's dog runs to see what's happening,
a host of starlings take wing, the tiger lilies are in flower
at the edge of the parking lot next to this house.
Professor, I don't suppose that you'd care to arm-wrestle?

JOE ROSENBLATT

b. 1933

Balloon Flowers

In the greenhouse
I'm staring down at pregnancies; tiny zeppelins—
skins: leopard
    clotted
        —soul's orgasm—bal
          loon flowers

                I reach out to touch
                I tickle their ear lobes
                rub the triggers
                of each
                        balloon flower, they
                        don't complain, but
                        blush out
                        at my fingers, o
                        what distilled
                        manures & minerals
                        nourished
                        these
                        air
                        brothels.
                        I'm staring at bellies
                        clotted with leopard:
                        zeppelins swelling out
                        happy
                        pregnancies. ALIEN
                          GLANDS,

they are not of this planet
these pregnancies: I touch
touch
fungus dreams, touch
passions of leopard
painted
on
blood
blood

blood

Mother Nature's Proletarians

Bees are truck drivers of the sky
who burrow into diners of flowers
to be fed therein, & overhauled.
"I'll try another flower", think the honey bees,
"taste so goddam delicious, this flower
ummmmm...such O, dour, & colour".
Buzzzzzzzzzzzzzzzzzzzzzzzzzz flip flip . .
Pregnant with proletarian bug song
they carry their freight of pollen groceries
home to Momma—the boss queen!

Bees are truck drivers of the sky
who buzz into diners
demanding lobotomies for breakfast:
waitresses of flies scatter
before the maniacs of proletarians
—each blossom becomes a delicious body house
for diesel dancers in the atmosphere
                              Bzzzzzzzzzzzzzzzzzzzzzzzzzzzzz
 zzzzzzzzzzzzzzzzzzzzzzzzzzzzzzzzzzzzzzzzzzzzzzzzzzzzzzzzzzzzzzzzzz
zzzzzzzz
          blip! blip! blip! blip! blip! blip! blip! blip!   zzzzz

```
zzzzzzzzzzzz sssssssssssssssssssssss zzzzzz blipblipblip zzzz
                                                             z
                                                             z
                                                             z
                                                             z
bizzzzzzzzzzzzzzzzzzzzzzzzzzzzzzzzzzzzzzzzzzzzzzzzzzzzzzzzzzzzz
zzzzzzzzzzzzzzzzzzzzzzzzzzzzzzzzzzzzzzzzzzzzzzzzzzzzzzzzzzzzzzz
zzzzzzzzzzzzzzzzzzzzzzzzzzzzzz        bizzzzzzzzzzzzzzzzzzzzzzz
bizzzzzzzzzzzzzzzzzzzzzzzzzz          bizzzzzzzzzzzzzzzzzzzzzzz
buzzzzzzzzzzzzzzzzzzzzzzzzz           zzzzzzzzzzzz  zzzzzzzzzzzz
bizzzzzz zzzzzzz  zzzzzzzz            zzzzzzz       zzzzzz
z
z                                                          z
z
z                                                            z
z
z                                                          z
z                                                            z
z
zzzzzzzzzzzzzzzzzzzzzzzzzzzzzzzzzzzzzzzzzzzzzzzzzzzzzzzzzzzzzzz
                    Bizzzzzzzzzzzzzzzzzzzzzzzz
                    z                    z
                    z
                    z                      z
                    z
                    z                        z
                    z
                    z                      z
                    b
                    z
                    z
                    z
                    z
                    z
                    z
                    b
                    e
                    z
                    z
                    z
                    z
                    z
                    z
                    z
```

```
z
z
z
z
z
z
 z
z        bees are, animal
 z       bees are, animal
z        bees are, animal
 z       bees are, animal
 z       bees are, animal
  z      bees are, animal
   z     bees are, animal
    z    bees are, animal
     z   bees are, animal
      z  bees are, animal
       z bees are, animal
        z bees are, animal
         z bees are, animal
          z bees are, animal
           z bees are, animal
            z bees are, animal
             z bees are, animal
               bees are, animal
               bees
               bees
               bees
               bees
               bees
               bees
               bees
               bees
               bees
```

Uncle Nathan Speaking from Landlocked Green

Wide, wide are the margins of sleep
deep, deep, deep in the flowerbox earth
I sleep .. sleep .. sleep ..
In Carp's ethereal tabernacle
micron lips crackle
spirit embryos gestate
grow jinx wings, umbilical fins, slit gills
cold heart, lung, and lizard's spine
as from a cyanide back bone
flux of shadows strum ... spiritons
from Death's encrusted harp.
Nephew, in this world
no dust remains, no nickel photos of our bones.
We are beyond dust
where spiritons and atoms hum
around a perfect planetary sun.
—such is spectral sex—
from worm to flourescent penetrant
in the grave, we all swing polar umbra.
Oye, so vengeful is Death's metamorphosis
that I go reincarnated in a minnow's whisper
who once dwelt as a barbaric fishmonger;
and now who can measure my sad physique?
or catch my whisper on a spectrograph.
Yet more soul pinching than worm's acetylene:
There is no commerce in the Netherworld.
Earth Momma, forgive me
for every fish I disembowelled was a child;
there is no Kaddish for aborted caviar.
Earth! Earth! is the bitch still green
liced with people and Aardvark powers?
And my shop on Baldwin street
does it stand? .. damp and sacred as the Wailing Wall
under the caterpillar'd canopy of God?
or has my neighbour swallowed up my Carp shrined
    enterprise
wherein I cradled images from Lake Genneserat

to fish fertiled ladies with halvah tongues
who shred my serpents into shrimp bread,
for fish food oscillates an old maid's chromosomes!
Carp, pickerel, transmogrified
where swimmers have been tranquilized
stomach's the body's palpitating madrigal.
God bless the primate's primeval stretch
but O to touch . . . touch . .
a moon's vibration of a silver dollar
to see the fish scales rise and fall
before Lent's locust of Friday's carnivores.
Nephew, heaven is on Earth; above me
the sky is smiling like a White fish.
Its eyes are the moon and the sun.

The Dream Apprentice

My spirit recalls its scherzo,
the diffident purples digging for their winter
to hide under the flaccid light.
The dream apprentice extracts the loud chemistry:
the puerile orange, yellow, purple.
His voice comes through a mound of dead dreams:
"This world is fertilizer for other worlds, miniatures."

He senses each blossom, enemies of chiaroscuro.
They irradiate on the cold spaces.
He cries, "You shall have no incinerator
before me, no other mother."

They become less than dwarfs, continually hungry
for passion & fast travel. How can they win the war?
Out there on a star ship he is neutral, dumb & powerful.

I close my eyes, fearful, that each dream
contains the roots of his hands, or his eyes.

I must be vigilant, the dream apprentice is a carnivore
who feeds his shadows all those deep deep dreamers.

Groundhogs & Appearances

O, we're blank.
Groundhogs fade into the roots of our eyes.
Once we could light fires with hallucinations
but now we just breathe lightly
& count our memories. Have we missed an important
     sensation?
Concrete images? Rabbit food?
Dare we lie down and sleep?
We're almost invisible.

Billions of rodent souls!
They've turned the System into a garbage dump,
but we're still buried alive in our bodies.

We'll close our eyes,
imagine the asterisks out in a private space.
Our images are double-parked out there.

FROM *The Brides of the Stream*

The fish is a fading mariner
with a monsoon in each eye.
He swims through a foam that sings
for fat wives and sex shinier than lures.

He hears the drum beat
from a trout holocaust.
He summons the survivors.
His fins stoke the fire.
Thousands of dark eyes haunt my hook.

*

The dead have arrived to enjoy my improper flies
skittering in the sun near a nimble-footed tee pee of a spider.
On a leaf, cool croupier, he deals libidinous pearls to his
gyrating lady.

I have selected a momentary fly. It has no true pilot's
heart, but lures like a woman of the night. Frothing like poor
emissaries at a generous state luncheon, stream munchkins
snap at a few woolen twists, animal hair, assorted fibres
glued to a ghoulish hook. My fly is sent out to drown in
circles. The false fly, an unmentionable molecule, is lost.

My mind closes like a Venus's Flytrap. Eyes smaller
than aquatic flies burn. A delicate white mouth opens. One
has to be guarded about gifts from strangers. Nathan seems
aware that my dry fly is not palatable. Again I coach my fly
in expectation of a primitive jaw moving quicker than a
grasssnake snapping a viridescent straddler. In the distance
the fanatic in me glows: I see an oblong pre-man,
proto-Christ gaffed on a treble hook.

Others have taken the lure, easy sex: *a bright fly on a
dark day*. I try another hors d'oeuvre. A green gondola dips
an engine in the shade. He refuses a phony grasshopper.

*

The energy finds its way back to the dreamer
to the dark side of the fish, your portion
and you cry, 'what is your name?'
but your shadow is silent . . .
the dark side follows you across the surface

The energy finds its way back to the fish
who is always drowning in a 'deep still pool'
My shadow divides into minnows
I was never there in the silence.

LEONARD COHEN

b. 1934

For Anne

With Annie gone,
Whose eyes to compare
With the morning sun?

Not that I did compare,
But I do compare
Now that she's gone.

I Have Not Lingered in European Monasteries

I have not lingered in European monasteries
and discovered among the tall grasses tombs of knights
who fell as beautifully as their ballads tell;

I have not parted the grasses
or purposefully left them thatched.

I have not released my mind to wander and wait
in those great distances
between the snowy mountains and the fishermen,
like a moon,
or a shell beneath the moving water.

I have not held my breath
so that I might hear the breathing of God,
or tamed my heartbeat with an exercise,
or starved for visions.

Although I have watched him often
I have not become the heron,
leaving my body on the shore,
and I have not become the luminous trout,
leaving my body in the air.

I have not worshipped wounds and relics,
or combs of iron,
or bodies wrapped and burnt in scrolls.

I have not been unhappy for ten thousand years.
During the day I laugh and during the night I sleep.
My favourite cooks prepare my meals,
my body cleans and repairs itself,
and all my work goes well.

Now of Sleeping

Under her grandmother's patchwork quilt
a calico bird's-eye view
of crops and boundaries
naming dimly the districts of her body
sleeps my Annie like a perfect lady

Like ages of weightless snow
on tiny oceans filled with light
her eyelids enclose deeply
a shade tree of birthday candles
one for every morning
until the now of sleeping

The small banner of blood
kept and flown by Brother Wind
long after the pierced bird fell down
is like her red mouth
among the squalls of pillow

Bearers of evil fancy
of dark intention and corrupting fashion
who come to rend the quilt
plough the eye and ground the mouth
will contend with mighty Mother Goose
and Farmer Brown and all good stories
of invincible belief
which surround her sleep
like the golden weather of a halo

Well-wishers and her true lover
may stay to watch my Annie
sleeping like a perfect lady
under her grandmother's patchwork quilt
but they must promise to whisper
and to vanish by morning—
all but her one true lover.

For E. J. P.

I once believed a single line
        in a Chinese poem could change
                forever how blossoms fell
and that the moon itself climbed on
        the grief of concise weeping men
                to journey over cups of wine
I thought invasions were begun for crows
        to pick at a skeleton
                dynasties sown and spent
to serve the language of a fine lament
        I thought governors ended their lives
                as sweetly drunken monks
telling time by rain and candles
        instructed by an insect's pilgrimage
                across the page—all this
so one might send an exile's perfect letter
to an ancient home-town friend

I chose a lonely country
	broke from love
		scorned the fraternity of war
I polished my tongue against the pumice moon
	floated my soul in cherry wine
		a perfumed barge for Lords of Memory
to languish on to drink to whisper out
	their store of strength
		as if beyond the mist along the shore
their girls their power still obeyed
	like clocks wound for a thousand years
I waited until my tongue was sore

Brown petals wind like fire around my poems
	I aimed them at the stars but
		like rainbows they were bent
before they sawed the world in half
	Who can trace the canyoned paths
		cattle have carved out of time
wandering from meadowlands to feasts
	Layer after layer of autumn leaves
		are swept away
Something forgets us perfectly

Style

I don't believe the radio stations
of Russia and America
but I like the music and I like
the solemn European voices announcing jazz
I don't believe opium or money
though they're hard to get
and punished with long sentences
I don't believe love
in the midst of my slavery I
do not believe
I am a man sitting in a house
on a treeless Argolic island

I will forget the grass of my mother's lawn
I know I will
I will forget the old telephone number
Fitzroy seven eight two oh
I will forget my style
I will have no style
I hear a thousand miles of hungry static
and the old clear water eating rocks
I hear the bells of mules eating
I hear the flowers eating the night
under their folds
Now a rooster with a razor
plants the haemophilia gash across
the soft black sky
and now I know for certain

I will forget my style
Perhaps a mind will open in this world
perhaps a heart will catch rain
Nothing will heal and nothing will freeze
but perhaps a heart will catch rain
America will have no style
Russia will have no style
It is happening in the twenty-eighth year
of my attention
I don't know what will become
of the mules with their lady eyes
or the old clear water
or the giant rooster
The early morning greedy radio eats
the governments one by one the languages
the poppy fields one by one
Beyond the numbered band
a silence develops for every style
for the style I laboured on
an external silence like the space
between insects in a swarm
electric unremembering
and it is aimed at us
(I am sleepy and frightened)
it makes toward me brothers

What I'm Doing Here

I do not know if the world has lied
I have lied
I do not know if the world has conspired against love
I have conspired against love
The atmosphere of torture is no comfort
I have tortured
Even without the mushroom cloud
still I would have hated

Listen
I would have done the same things
even if there were no death
I will not be held like a drunkard
under the cold tap of facts
I refuse the universal alibi

Like an empty telephone booth passed at night
and remembered
like mirrors in a movie palace lobby consulted
only on the way out
like a nymphomaniac who binds a thousand
into strange brotherhood
I wait
for each one of you to confess

Two Went to Sleep

Two went to sleep
almost every night
one dreamed of mud
one dreamed of Asia
visiting a zeppelin
visiting Nijinsky

Two went to sleep
one dreamed of ribs
one dreamed of senators
Two went to sleep
two travellers
The long marriage
in the dark
The sleep was old
the travellers were old
one dreamed of oranges
one dreamed of Carthage
Two friends asleep
years locked in travel
Good night my darling
as the dreams waved goodbye
one travelled lightly
one walked through water
visiting a chess game
visiting a booth
always returning
to wait out the day
One carried matches
one climbed a beehive
one sold an earphone
one shot a German
Two went to sleep
every sleep went together
wandering away
from an operating table
one dreamed of grass
one dreamed of spokes
one bargained nicely
one was a snowman
one counted medicine
one tasted pencils
one was a child
one was a traitor
visiting heavy industry
visiting the family

Two went to sleep
none could foretell
one went with baskets
one took a ledger
one night happy
one night in terror
Love could not bind them
Fear could not either
they went unconnected
they never knew where
always returning
to wait out the day
parting with kissing
parting with yawns
visiting Death till
they wore out their welcome
visiting Death till
the right disguise worked   1964

Untitled Poem

Any system you contrive without us
will be brought down
We warned you before
and nothing that you built has stood
Hear it as you lean over your blueprint
Hear it as you roll up your sleeve
Hear it once again
Any system you contrive without us
will be brought down
You have your drugs
You have your guns
You have your Pyramids and your Pentagons
With all your grass and bullets
you cannot hunt us any more
All that we disclose of ourselves forever
is this warning

Nothing that you built has stood
Any system you contrive without us
will be brought down

Untitled Poem

Welcome to these lines
There is a war on
but I'll try to make you comfortable
Don't follow my conversation
it's just nervousness
Didn't I make love to you
when we were students of the East
Yes the house is different
the village will be taken soon
I've removed whatever
might give comfort to the enemy
We are alone
until the times change
and those who have been betrayed
come back like pilgrims to this moment
when we did not yield
and call the darkness poetry

GEORGE BOWERING

b. 1935

Radio Jazz

Sucked into the horn of the jazz
on lonely midnight Salt Lake City radio
over to me alone in a big house
hundreds of miles in the mountains
fantastic piano then
key to me right hand left hand on silent radio sound
on a million radio America waves in the dark

Folks all gone folks
gone to the Coast leaving me and
the shelf radio in hot night kitchen
old 'riends gone home three empty cups on the table here
Gerry Mulligan meets Stan Getz
in the next one in the last one
on the radio award bandstand
down away on the truck coming road
sound radio bound Salt Lake City comes on

August, 1961

Grandfather

Grandfather
            Jabez Harry Bowering
strode across the Canadian prairie
hacking down trees
               and building churches
delivering personal baptist sermons in them
leading Holy holy holy lord god almighty songs in them
red haired man squared off in the pulpit
reading Saul on the road to Damascus at them

Left home
            big walled Bristol town
at age eight
             to make a living
buried his stubby fingers in root snarled earth
for a suit of clothes and seven hundred gruelly meals a year
taking an anabaptist cane across the back every day
for four years till he was whipped out of England

Twelve years old
             and across the ocean alone
to apocalyptic Canada
                 Ontario of bone bending child labor
six years on the road to Damascus till his eyes were blinded
with the blast of Christ and he wandered west
to Brandon among wheat kings and heathen Saturday nights
young red haired Bristol boy shoveling coal
in the basement of Brandon college five in the morning

Then built his first wooden church and married
a sick girl who bore two live children and died
leaving several pitiful letters and the Manitoba night

He moved west with another wife and built children and
    churches
Saskatchewan Alberta British Columbia Holy holy holy
lord god almighty
                         struck his labored bones with pain
and left him a postmaster prodding grandchildren with
    crutches
another dead wife and a glass bowl of photographs
and holy books unopened save the bible by the bed

Till he died the day before his eighty fifth birthday
in a Catholic hospital of sheets white as his hair

The Night Before Morning

With it all over
and you & I
in separate beds
in separated houses,

I think of
Troilus & Cressida
cursing the sun—
rise from their hurricaned bed;

he to clatter away
on his army horse,
she to pick
her sunny way home—

you & I
with nothing touching
but our private thoughts:
mine of poetry,
yours of a strong morning.

Esta Muy Caliente

On the highway
near San Juan del Río
we had to stop the car
for a funeral.

The whole town it was
a hundred people or
two hundred
walking slowly along the highway

toward the yellow domed church
on the top of the hill
and we pulled into the shade
of a shaggy tree.

I turned off the engine
and we heard their music
a screeching saxophone
and high broken noted trumpet

alone and sad in the hot afternoon
as they walked slow like sheep
the women with black shawls
the men in flappy trousers.

Every five minutes the men
threw cherry bombs into the air
behind them: loud gun shots
blasting the afternoon

then the saxophone: tin music
odd tortured jazz
in that mysterious Indian Christian march
up the hill: bearing a coffin to the priest.

It was a small coffin
on the shoulder of one man in front
        the father we thought
the cherry bombs were like violence

against us: but we were stopped.
An old rattling truck
nosed thru them: and they closed
together again behind it
                            ignoring us.

I walked away from the road
in among the bushes and prickly pear
looking for scorpions on the hot sand
and took a leak beside a thin horse.

An hour later the road was clear
and as I got in the car
a man on a donkey came by
a San Juan lonely in the mountains man.

Good afternoon, I said.
Good afternoon, he said, it is very hot.
Yes it is, I said, especially for us.
It is very hot for us too, he said.

Circus Maximus

They come
            each one
of them
        a rise
like those
           who came
before them.

New heroes flexing
to fill the shape
made out for them
by the now dead

but each new man
a refutation of his predecessor.

Camus refining Dostoyevsky
yet feeling the swell
of body the Russian felt

the old man
grizzling in his beard
anticipating the African
who would fit his fingers
over the old pen
playing with down
           on his cheek.

Who knows ten of your molecules
are not in me?

but Nature helps me define
my own shape

looks on as
I stumble over the centuries'
exposed root
lost in my own
                    particularity

(patterns I deny
and that
is part of a pattern).

Styles do not multiply themselves
but are all
pervasive

the suit of clothes
is nothing
without its own disfigurations.

New heroes flex into it
and bend it to their bodies.

Inside the Tulip

Inside the tulip
we make love
on closer look
seeing faint green lines, new

Let me share this flower
with you, kiss you
press my tongue on pollen
against the roof of my mouth

Look at me long enough
and I will be a flower
or wet blackberries dangling
from a dripping bush

Let me share you
with this flower, look
at anything long enough
and it is water

on a leaf, a petal
where we lie, bare legs together

Daphne Marlatt

        In the midst of her sorrow she was
pisst off.
        I always thought if I ever took her
wrist between my finger & thumb it might
snap. But that she can get pisst off, & in
her writing.
        I always thought the words snapt from
her one by one, twigs the birds rested
on & when they flew someone snapt them
off.
        But inside her head there is a torrent. It
is enough to step into that & bathe.
        (In the bath she must be remarkable among
the white procelain
                & what does she do with
that long wiry black hair with white strands
running thru?)
        Lately the sorrow is no longer borne & her
body is discovered not to be brittle & her
voice tells you she is pisst off but it has a
little too much humor in it, a thin strand of
that, inside out sorrow.
        In 1960 she had black pedal-pushers & she
lookt so brittle I thought how does she move her
knees, is it painful, & then in 1965 the poems—
how could you follow them without breaking
your tongue.

Even then no one knew she was pisst off,
she didnt know because women didnt really
know & she made poems that were questions
stretcht out in space, ready to be snapt off.
Now you should hear her shout. It
is as if a stick had come alive in your hand.

Did

One thousand icebergs
in the sunlight around
the corner of New-
foundland, I saw

from the window
of a VC 10.
& wisht William Blake
could have seen that.

I did,

he said.

Against Description

I went to the blackberries
on the vine.

They were blackberries
on the vine.

They were
blackberries.

Black
berries.

JOHN NEWLOVE

b. 1938

The Flowers

It is raining, rain
streaks down the window to my left,
cars sluice water in the gutters
in the night, the round
neon clock-containing sign
hanging outside beside my window
sways in the wind and buzzes.

The flowers sprout everywhere,
in pots and boxes, on lawns
and trees, in gardens and ditches
the flowers are growing; the wet
wind will nourish them, cut
some down but feed the rest.

The sign crackles
and swings on its bar,
iron bar; the cars go by
all the night. They cut
a momentary trail and mark,
disappearing, on the wet
black pavement. The cars go by,
the police in their cars
prowl restlessly
up and down the rainy avenue
looking for interlopers, anyone
afoot at night in the rain,
the blue and dangerous
gun-hipped cops.

The car came smashing
and wrecking his face, his head,
poor hit hurt head
bleeding on the roadway
and in the cool hospital
night in bandages
and glued-on tape.

His eyes, they said,
were soft and easy
years ago. Now
he wears them cleverly
like some secret
coupled badge,
twin and original, dark
ice eyes that watch and assess
slowly what they have
fixed
on; his head does not move.

In the hospitals
with antiseptic nurses
stripping him, knife-
fisted surgeons bending down,

they cut, irony,
to save his life; and he stayed
days and years filled
with tantalizing drugs, interminable
dreams, tangled in bandages and
shocks, suspicions, a nonchalant
profusion of hopes and cures,
surrounded by the tears
of his rainy crazy peers.

Rain, wind, and spring, all things
drove him crazy and grow
flowers, flowers
that dance in the rain,
the bulging flowers that grew
in his head, plants
of evil or god, some
holy epileptic angel, bloated
inhuman flowers shining
their bright colours
insistently, turning
slowly in the wind
and spring, tortuous
creaking growths, thick
cancerous things
in the rain, stems
like the barrels of rifles,
fat lead bullet roots
gripping the damp earth.

And the cars
pass up and down
the streets, disappearing
trails, the blue police
pass, coughing
behind their leathery fists,
guns dangling
from their hips, eyes
watching. My flowery clock
buzzes and mutters,
typewriter taps
like the rain. I breathe
as harshly as the wind.

Samuel Hearne in Wintertime

1.

In this cold room
I remember the smell of manure
on men's heavy clothes as good,
the smell of horses.

It is a romantic world
to readers of journeys
to the Northern Ocean—

especially if their houses are heated
to some degree, Samuel.

Hearne, your camp must have smelled
like hell whenever you settled down
for a few days of rest and journal-work:

hell smeared with human manure,
hell half-full of raw hides,
hell of sweat, Indians, stale fat,
meat-hell, fear-hell, hell of cold.

2.

One child is back from the doctor's while
the other one wanders about in dirty pants
and I think of Samuel Hearne and the land—

puffy children coughing as I think,
crying, sick-faced,
vomit stirring in grey blankets
from room to room.

It is Christmastime—
the cold flesh shines.
No praise in merely enduring.

3.

Samuel Hearne did more
in the land (like all the rest

full of rocks and hilly country,
many very extensive tracts of land,
tittimeg, pike and barble,

and the islands:
the islands, many
of them abound

as well as the main
land does
with dwarf woods,

chiefly pine
in some parts intermixed
with larch and birch) than endure.

The Indians killed twelve deer.
It was impossible to describe
the intenseness of the cold.

4.

And, Samuel Hearne,
I have almost begun to talk

as if you wanted to be
gallant, as if you went
through that land for a book—

as if you were not SAM, wanting
to know, to do a job.

5.

There was that Eskimo girl
at Bloody Falls, at your feet,

Samuel Hearne, with two spears in her,
you helpless before your helpers,

and she twisted about them like
an eel, dying, never to know.

Crazy Riel

Time to write a poem
or something.
Fill up a page.
The creature noise.
Huge massed forces of men
hating each other.
What young men do not know.
To keep quiet,
contemporaneously.
Contempt. The robin diligently
on the lawn sucks up worms,
hopping from one to another.
Youthfully. Sixteen miles
from my boyhood home
the frogs sit in the grassy marsh
that looks like a golf course
by the lake. Green frogs.
Boys catch them for bait or sale.
Or caught them. Time.
To fill up a page.
To fill up a hole.
To make things feel better. Noise.
The noise of the images
that are people I will never understand.
Admire them though I may.

Poundmaker. Big Bear. Wandering Spirit,
those miserable men.
Riel. Crazy Riel. Riel hanged.
Politics must have its way.
The way of noise. To fill up.
The definitions bullets make,
and field guns.
The noise your dying makes,
to which you are the only listener.
The noise the frogs hesitate
to make as the metal hook
breaks through the skin
and slides smoothly into place
in the jaw. The noise
the fish makes caught in the jaw,
which is only an operation
of the body and the element,
which a stone would make
thrown in the same water, thrashing,
not its voice.
The lake is not displaced
with one less jackfish body.
In the slough that looks like a golf course
the family of frogs sings. Metal throats.
The images of death hang upside-down.
Grey music.
It is only the listening for death,
fingering the paraphernalia,
the noise of the men you admire.
And cannot understand.
Knowing little enough about them.
The knowledge waxing.
The wax that paves hell's road,
slippery as the road to heaven.
So that as a man slips
he might as easily slide
into being a saint as destroyer.
In his ears the noise magnifies.
He forgets men.

The Prairie

One compiles, piles, plies
these masses of words, verbs,
massifs, mastiffs barking meaning,
dried chips
of buffalo dung, excreta from beasts

the prairie fed, foddered,
food for generations: men roaming
as beasts seen through dips
in history, fostered by legend,
invented remembrance. Scenes shake,

the words do not suffice. One bred
on the same earth wishes himself
something different, the other's
twin, impossible thing, twining
both memories, a double meaning,

but cannot be—never
to be at ease, but always migrating
from city to city
seeking some almost seen
god or food or earth or word.

The Cave

The stars are your deathbed.
You rest from the cave
to Pluto or whatever dark planets
lie beyond. No ideas trap you.

In the unobstructed sunlight miles high
the Earth is beautiful as a postcard.
Sinai looks as the map says it should,
and people are too small to be observed.

In Africa there are no trees to see.
It is a map world.
The sunlight is brilliant
as a two-carat diamond on a girl's hand.

The girl is young, visible to your mind,
growing older. Beyond Pluto
and the darkest planets, children surround her.

The diamond glows on her finger
like a worm. The stars, the stars
shine like one-carat diamonds. Beyond
Pluto and the darkest planets the stars shine.

The diamonds shine in wormy rings
on fingers, in coffins of unobstructed space.
The flesh circles the bone in strips
in the coffin as the ring circled flesh.

The two-carat sun hangs loosely,
just restraining the Earth. Beyond the planets,
beyond the dark coffin, beyond the ring of stars,
your bed is in the shining, tree-lit cave.

Harry, 1967

Old Harry just sits on the porch all day staring at himself
        and not seeing a damn thing.

Or to tell the truth he doesn't even sit on the porch. His
        house hasn't got a porch.

Or to tell the truth Harry hasn't got a house.

Harry lives in a ten-dollar-a-week light-housekeeping room
        and thinks of himself sitting on the porch of a house
        he never had.

Harry has become very familiar with oatmeal and macaroni
in his old age. He is thirty-six, born in 1931.

Born after the First World War, born after the twenties, born
just in time to barely remember a small portion of the
Depression, born too young to fight in the Second
World War, to remember details really well.

Harry is five foot seven and a half, Harry weighs
one hundred and thirty pounds, Harry has dandruff,
Harry has bad teeth and no prospect of ever getting
them fixed, Harry wears glasses, Harry quit school
at sixteen before he finished Grade Nine to get in on
the big money.

Harry looks like he's had TB all his life but Harry hasn't,
Harry has nothing and looks like getting less.

But Harry sits on that porch all day feeling the sunlight
almost and not seeing a damn thing. It's been a lousy
life and it's only just half over.

Harry is thirty-six and he doesn't even dream about women
anymore. Harry knows he'll never touch a woman again.

So what's the use of thinking about it.

But Harry used to see things.

Harry went to Ethiopia and was a general in a revolution.

And he killed the emperor with his own hand.

And his gallant tribesmen swept down upon the lines of
khaki machine-gunmen and sabred every one of them.

Harry was nicked by a fragment of shell that left an
inch-long cut like one a knife would make on
his forearm.

And Harry had no expression on his face when he removed
  the cigarette from his mouth and used its burning tip
  to cauterize the wound while fat newspapermen gasped
  in admiration as the faint smell of toasted flesh
  reached them.

And the movie cameras whirred.

And Harry waved his sword and ordered his cavalry to
  charge and all around the world movie audiences
  watching the Movietone News gasped as Harry
  slaughtered the old Emperor himself and his admiring
  tribesmen crowned Harry king and Harry . . .

Harry always thought the word was calvary not cavalry,
  legacy of a short time at Sunday School in the damp
  cloakroom of a prairie United Church.

That was a long time ago to Harry and he has a long time
  to go.

And Harry doesn't see anymore.

He doesn't know that it's useless to see things that can never
  happen, he doesn't know that for him dreaming is just
  a lie now, that seeing things is no good for him, too
  late: that isn't why Harry doesn't see.

Harry just can't anymore, that's all.

Notes From and Among the Wars

1

Your drink is twice as strong as mine is
Your mouth is twice as fair as mine is
Your hair is sweeter than mine is
You smile where I could wish to smile
You sleep when I could wish to sleep

I wish to dream, I wish to dream
through our centuries of blood

2

Dead arrogant kings
    bearded in gold
beautiful to archaeologists
living on slaves slaves—
    my people
having come out of Asia
your sons the seven Osmanli mutes
    who strangle and smile
what have you done
but bow and wait
for the petty lords of creation
heirs of the floods and the plagues
    and dead with gold
a crust on the rotted faces
till you after some centuries or so
could use a new plow to conquer Europe?

3

Were the bunks neat in Auschwitz?
Was the soul's blond efficiency repulsed
by the messy blankets of Jews and Gypsies?—If
they had blankets, those who surrendered
immortal teeth of gold, surrendered rings, piles
of prosthetics tabulated in the avenues
between the wooden huts, and all else?

4

In the end you don't even know yourself
only the hill you must climb; but not even
the hill; a bump on it, one hump of grass
a flint, a blade thin in the wind as you climb
each step, each breath taken in a dissimilar time

5

And how after each little separation
we seem to have to learn again
to know each other as awkward strangers do—
the slightest kiss our accidental hands our eyes
that waver off each other as if we had not been
nakedly in love

6

I would like to whistle softly in your ear
to recall to you a tune we might have played
if I could remember it. Instead I sit reading
of man's perpetual wars,
of how he says he strides toward the stars

7

Among the wars
the poet walks along
in his mind
from the start
gone wrong
unable to find
some simple part
that he might make
into an easy song
or phrase to take
as medicine
when he walks along
in his mind,

when his mind soars
from the start,
gone wrong

8

And to see men
attempting to do things
and their women
wary, protecting them,
wolves distrusting all strangers,
smiling like guards

9

As among the wars
and fears
we sail
or kill—
wanderers. . . .

10

And what one would have thought
to have brought forward
to build on
                has become one's life,
with no addition

11

Movie

There's a man inside there, dying
as you in your homogalactic excitement watch
the fuming awkward plane
fifty-five funny years ago
dive in twisty smoke
into a poison sea of shell-ploughed earth:
it is a movie.

       For you it would be much more bitter
just to walk in the streets
than to watch those older deaths again

12

Today when the sun does not rise
Today when the rulers cannot stop the snow
Today as the murders cross the screen
Today as the headlines are hopelessly accepted
Today watching a real-life neo-gothic fistfight
Today on the outskirts of no novel
Today during the shakiness of human life
Today during our constant killing ignorance
declaring our deaths in continuous rehearsal
we live and try to love —

                    ourselves at least,
if no others

  13

The green trees grow from year to year
and seem to have no thoughts
although I hear it said
they scream when we kill before them

  14

And give us a little pity too:
for the last drink in the whisky bottle
sunday afternoon, for the calcium in our spines
for the daily prejudiced paper, the constant liars
those who think war is a high-school debate
the ones who take freedom away
in the name of freedom
as our portions get smaller

Forgive us: for whom civilization consists of acquiring
the correct mental addictions, those of us who act
as if we hated the human in ourselves
knowing there is enough to hate
in the human in ourselves

The wars the slaveries no dead men redeemed by poems
no humiliation redressed with songs
no chain scars in the soul erased with apologies
a hundred years late
the simple everyday savagery of parent to child
or child to parent brother to brother sister to sister

The torture goes on forever as we in perpetual motion
breed and destroy ourselves for any reason
even intelligent ones

All of which we have always known
in despair and amusement at ourselves

15

And there is an egypt of the mind
grotesque mysterious remote
sacrificial
where the dunes are piling and unpiling
their arabesques coiling about some point
not grasped some
secret living to be learned
desperately longed for. . . .

Blue and green commingling, the muscley sea
sliding through the mind, a notion of deeper rivers
than those that run over the earth, among the stars
currents in the bright mixture pulsing, something
that might be there to save us as it seems
we cannot save ourselves or do not want to. . . .

16

To be willingless, to be willing. . . .

Willingless and willing. as when
the pickup truck went around
a slight curve to the right
years ago and stopped. Off the road
a small triangular piece of level ground
a wooden shack a quick shallow river
and then the trees again as far as could be seen
night coming thoughts of bears the sound
of crisp leaves as bits of wind brushed off them
a place unknown and feared
and the driver saying This
is as far as I go
meaning this is as far as you go. . . .

17

But what should we expect of our memories
except remembrance? We who are so adept
so practised in false hopes so able to read
the slightest changes in a face
the slightest intonations in a voice
the indications of things
that do not exist affirmations
never considered by the other. . . .

18

But me? Waking up mornings
my mouth full of blood
it seeming to be such a difficult life
and yet so easy not to be
as water rings in the musical hillside sewers
in a false Spring
hoarding regrets

And the ghost that sings in my blood
a mortal
everything waiting for its boat-shaped grave ender
of the sad tricks we play on ourselves
ender of foolish lives
and foolish loves greatly desired ending
the crying instruments of speech
that repeat and repeat themselves happily repeating
the past from which they are trying to rise

19

You smile where I could wish to smile
You sleep when I could wish to sleep. . . .
It is not the milk-bearing tree I see
but the one that seeps blood or trees
exploding like tnt in the winter's cold

20

Caught in the maze of life
and knowing only that we end

Avoiding infinity
with questions

Was I a lover you had
out of your kindliness
in wintertime?

Is today the day I got old?

Is today the day you got old?
And were only able to sing a structured song?
So—

If you were in the air
would you be a bird?

If you were able
would you wish to be?
And would you sing
if you wished to be?
And if you cared to be —

Would you want to fly? knowing
below and as you fly
in the green concealed pit
the hunters with their sighted shotguns lie.

That There Is No Relaxation

A little more and a little more.
Shining lines stifle me.
Let us have icons.
Cheap cast metal twisted.
That which computers do.
On a beach, cramped, the dead flesh clawing.
No relaxation in death.
There is an image for it.
A little more and a little more.
Let me have it.
Red against blue ice.
It is all ice.
It is all ice.
Give me hard-hearted women.
To dream about.
Lord?
No images.
A little more and a little more.
To dream about.
Am I crazy?
Give me nothing.
Nothing to dream about.
Lord. Don't listen to me.
A little more and a little more.

[handwritten: Post Modern writer]

MARGARET ATWOOD

b. 1939

[handwritten: m.p. to T.S. Elliot.]

[handwritten: — Mythological character → a prophetess → an oracle.]

[handwritten: - faith just isn't enough we need proof of Truth.]

A Sibyl

Below my window
in the darkening
backyard the children
play at war
among the flowerbeds

on my shelves the bottles
accumulate
         my sibyl (every woman
         should have one) has chosen
         to live there

thin green wine bottles
emptied of small dinners
ovaltine jars, orange-brown
emptied of easy sleep

         my sibyl crouches
         in one of them
         wrinkled as a pickled
         baby, twoheaded prodigy
         at a freakfair
         hairless, her sightless
         eyes like eggwhites

I stand looking
over the fading city

she calls to me with the many
voices of the children
not I want to die
but You must die
later or sooner alas
you were born weren't you
the minutes thunder like guns
coupling won't help you
or plurality
I see it
I prophesy

but she doesn't reach me.
Old spider
sibyl, I'll
uncork you
let in a little air
or I'll ignore you.

Right now
my skin is a sack of
clever tricks, five
senses ribboned like birthday presents unravel
in a torn web around me

and a man dances
in my kitchen, moving
like a metronome
with hopes of staying
for breakfast in the half-empty
bottle in his pocket

There are omens of
rockets among the tricycles
I know it

time runs out
in the ticking hips of the
man whose twitching skull
jerks on loose
vertebrae in my kitchen
flower
beds predict it

the city burns with an
afterglow of explosions as the
streetlights all come on

The thing that calls itself
I
right now
doesn't care
I don't care

I leave that to my
necessary sibyl
(that's what she's for)
with her safely bottled
anguish and her glass
despair

Some Objects of Wood and Stone

i) Totems

We went to the park
where they kept the wooden people:
static, multiple
uprooted and trans-
planted.

Their faces were restored,
freshly-painted.
In front of them
the other wooden people
posed for each other's cameras
and nearby a new booth
sold replicas and souvenirs.

One of the people was real.
It lay on its back, smashed
by a toppling fall or just
the enduring of minor winters.
Only one of the heads had
survived intact, and it was
also beginning to decay
but there was a
life in the progressing
of old wood back to
the earth, obliteration

that the clear-hewn
standing figures lacked.

As for us, perennial watchers,
tourists of another kind
there is nothing for us to worship;
no pictures of ourselves, no blue-
sky summer fetishes, no postcards
we can either buy, or
smiling
be.

There are few totems that remain
living for us.
Though in passing,
through glass we notice

dead trees in the seared meadows
dead roots bleaching in the swamps.

ii) Pebbles

Talking was difficult. Instead
we gathered coloured pebbles
from the places on the beach
where they occurred.

They were sea-smoothed, sea-completed.
They enclosed what they intended
to mean in shapes
as random and necessary
as the shapes of words

and when finally
we spoke
the sounds of our voices fell
into the air   single and
solid and rounded and really
there
and then dulled, and then like sounds
gone,   a fistful of gathered
pebbles there was no point
in taking home, dropped on a beachful
of other coloured pebbles

and when we turned to go
a flock of small
birds flew scattered by the
fright of our sudden moving
and disappeared: hard

sea pebbles
thrown solid for an instant
against the sky

flight of words

iii) Carved Animals

The small carved
animal is passed from
hand to hand
around the circle
until the stone grows warm

touching, the hands do not know
the form of animal
which was made or
the true form of stone
uncovered

and the hands, the fingers the
hidden small bones
of the hands bend to hold the shape,
shape themselves, grow
cold with the stone's cold, grow
also animal, exchange
until the skin wonders
if stone is human

In the darkness later
and even when the animal
has gone, they keep
the image of that
inner shape

hands holding warm
hands holding
the half-formed air

from the Circle Game.

Via negativa

This Is a Photograph of Me

It was taken some time ago.
At first it seems to be
a smeared
print: blurred lines and grey flecks
blended with the paper;

then, as you scan
it, you see in the left-hand corner
a thing that is like a branch: part of a tree
(balsam or spruce) emerging
and, to the right, halfway up
what ought to be a gentle
slope, a small frame house.

In the background there is a lake,
and beyond that, some low hills.

(The photograph was taken
the day after I drowned.

I am in the lake, in the center
of the picture, just under the surface.

It is difficult to say where
precisely, or to say
how large or small I am:
the effect of water
on light is a distortion

but if you look long enough,
eventually
you will be able to see me.)

The Animals in That Country

In that country the animals
have the faces of people:

Imag. Reality

the ceremonial
cats possessing the streets

the fox run
politely to earth, the huntsmen
standing around him, fixed
in their tapestry of manners

American

the bull, embroidered
with blood and given
an elegant death, trumpets, his name
stamped on him, heraldic brand
because

(when he rolled
on the sand, sword in his heart, the teeth
in his blue mouth were human)

he is really a man

even the wolves, holding resonant
conversations in their
forests thickened with legend.

In this country the animals
have the faces of
animals.

Real Reality

Their eyes
flash once in car headlights
and are gone.

canadian

Their deaths are not elegant.

They have the faces of
no-one.

A Night in the Royal Ontario Museum

Who locked me

into this crazed man-made
stone brain
           where the weathered
totempole jabs a blunt
finger at the byzantine
mosaic dome

Under that ornate
golden cranium I wander
among fragments of gods, tarnished
coins, embalmed gestures
chronologically arranged,
looking for the EXIT sign

but in spite of the diagrams
at every corner, labelled
in red: YOU ARE HERE
the labyrinth holds me,

turning me around
the cafeteria, the washrooms,
a spiral through marble
Greece and Rome, the bronze
horses of China

then past the carved masks, wood and fur
to where 5 plaster Indians
in a glass case
squat near a dusty fire

and further, confronting me
with a skeleton child, preserved
in the desert air, curled
beside a clay pot and a few beads.

I say I am far
enough,   stop here   please
no more

but the perverse museum, corridor
by corridor, an idiot
voice jogged by a pushed
button, repeats its memories

and I am dragged to the mind's
deadend, the roar of the bone-
yard, I am lost
among the mastodons
and beyond: a fossil
shell, then

samples of rocks
and minerals, even the thundering
tusks dwindling to pin-
points in the stellar
fluorescent-lighted
wastes of geology

Progressive Insanities of a Pioneer

I

He stood, a point
on a sheet of green paper
proclaiming himself the centre,

with no walls, no borders
anywhere; the sky no height
above him, totally un-
enclosed
and shouted:

Let me out!

II

He dug the soil in rows,
imposed himself with shovels.
He asserted
into the furrows, I
am not random.

The ground
replied with aphorisms:

a tree-sprout, a nameless
weed, words
he couldn't understand.

III

The house pitched
the plot staked
in the middle of nowhere.

At night the mind
inside, in the middle
of nowhere.

The idea of an animal
patters across the roof.

In the darkness the fields
defend themselves with fences
in vain:
        everything
        is getting in.

- imigrant Migration theme
- when you do find truth you
  will go insane.

IV

By daylight he resisted.
He said, disgusted
with the swamp's clamourings and the outbursts
of rocks,
>   This is not order
>   but the absence
>   of order.

He was wrong, the unanswering
forest implied:

>   It was
>   an ordered absence

V

For many years
he fished for a great vision,
dangling the hooks of sown
roots under the surface
of the shallow earth.

It was like
enticing whales with a bent
pin. Besides he thought

in that country
only the worms were biting.

VI

If he had known unstructured
space is a deluge
and stocked his log house-
boat with all the animals

even the wolves,

he might have floated.

But obstinate he
stated, The land is solid
and stamped,

watching his foot sink
down through stone
up to the knee.

VII

Things
refused to name themselves; refused
to let him name them.

The wolves hunted
outside.

On his beaches, his clearings,
by the surf of under-
growth breaking
at his feet, he foresaw
disintegration
                    and in the end
through eyes
made ragged by his
effort, the tension
between subject and object,

the green
vision, the unnamed
whale invaded.

There Is Only One of Everything

Not a tree but the tree
we saw, it will never exist, split by the wind
                    and bending down
like that again. What will push out of the earth

later, making it summer, will not be
grass, leaves, repetition, there will
have to be other words. When my

eyes close language vanishes. The cat
with the divided face, half black half orange
nests in my scruffy fur coat, I drink tea,

fingers curved around the cup, impossible
to duplicate these flavours. The table
and freak plates glow softly, consuming themselves,

I look out at you and you occur
in this winter kitchen, random as trees or sentences,
entering me, fading like them, in time you will disappear

but the way you dance by yourself
on the tile floor to a worn song, flat and mournful,
so delighted, spoon waved in one hand, wisps of
                    roughened hair

sticking up from your head, it's your surprised
body, pleasure I like, I can even say it,
though only once and it won't

last: I want this. I want
this.

After Jaynes

The old queen's head cut off
at the neck, then skinned & emptied,
boiled, coated with plaster,
cheeks and lips dyed red,
bright stones in the eyes

      After this transformation
      she can sing,
      can tell us what we think
      we need to hear

      This is 'poetry', this song
      of the wind across teeth,
      this message from the flayed tongue
      to the flayed ear

Trainride, Vienna-Bonn

   i

It's those helmets we remember,
the shape of a splayed cranium,
and the faces under them,
ruthless & uniform

But these sit on the train
clean & sane, in their neutral
beige & cream: this girl smiles,
she wears a plastic butterfly, and the waiter gives
a purple egg to my child
for fun. Kindness abounds.

ii

Outside the windows the trees flow
past in a tender mist,
lightgreen & moist with buds

What I see though is the black trunks,
a detail from Breughel:
the backs of three men returning
from the hunt, their hounds following,
stark lines against the snow.

iii

The forest is no darker
than any forests, my own
included, the fields we pass
could be my fields; except
for what the eye puts there.

In this field there is a man
running, and three others, chasing,
their brown coats
flapping against their boots.

Among the tree roots the running man
stumbles and is thrown
face down and stays there.

iv

What holds me
in the story we've all heard
so many times before:

the few who resisted,
who did not do what they were told.

This is the old fear:
not what can be done to you
but what you might do
yourself, or fail to.

This is the old torture.

v

three men in dark archaic
coats, their backs to me, returning
home to food and a good fire,
joking together, their hounds following.

This forest is alien
to me, closer than skin,
unknown, something early
as caves and buried, hard,

a chipped stone knife, the
long bone lying in darkness
inside my right arm: not
innocent but latent.

bill bissett

b. 1939

tell me what attackd yu

    th green broom
    i criticizd him
    most peopul have been led to believe
by th emergd middul class, that art
and politikal involvment greet each othr
only across sum imponderabul chasm,
    th middul class sz yeah its a good pome
    but what use is it, th professors
lift up our hearts, in repudiation of that,
to th credo that art transcends use, either
view is nowhere, art is all use; only
th technicians of a fragmented society,
    interested in propagating such a nightmare
    encourage us to belive in realities
    that split our breath into filing cards, p
for politiks, a for art—th full breath
is what knowledge is, is human, is
wholly real, includes what is
    in all things

Th Canadian

On th train, back from th Empress
dining car, snowing woodlands
  ,pulling thru Manitoba, recall
  how sum yrs after th second centenary
of th founding of Halifax, which
  date i commemorated with sign
  above my father's street door,
  into two parts i divided, th half
on th left, what once was, before
1749, th MicMac Indian, th second
half, after that time, a British sailor,
on board, telescope to eye, sailing
  into harbor, Montbatten drove by
  my father's house that day, part of
th ceremonies, dressd by University gown
& cap, later that year, th woman to be
Queen, then Princess Elizabeth drove
  thru Halifax town, in bullet-proof car.

But i was to recall, as i did,
coming back from th dining car, that
sum yrs after Halifax had her bicentenary,
i wrote my third or fourth pome, in
which, constructed as allegory, i did en
vision th society of fact in Canada
as a train, its peopuls classd, & sub-
classd, according to th rank & station,
that is, what they cud claim they owned, or,
who they cud claim owned them, its
peopuls cut off from each other by
  such coach cars & compartments.

And, i recall, part of th allegory, was
th train going thr th tunnel—darkness,
fortifying th condition, keeping each in place,
lest they overcome fear & th structure toppul.

It's not sucha good allegory, my
friends sd—well, now that sum of my best
friends are in jail—i see its uses,
   my boyhood despair—seeing, as th
   train rolls thru Manitoba, how it
does seem that still peopul are hungry in
this country, sum of my best friends are
   hungry, peopul are hungry, they hunger
for food—outside of this train there is
   no food—in it there is good & bad food,
   food that will just keep yu strong enuff
      to keep yr place—food that is
      just good enuff yu dream
         of better food—and food that is so good
      yu become encouraged to accept
         that this train is not going to crash
         cannot be changed, from within
         or without, is God or Allah's very
         handiwork, but where is th food
            on this train, this one
            to show me Allah in all things,
               for then, in ourselves th best food,
               we share th bounty
                  on this Iron Horse.

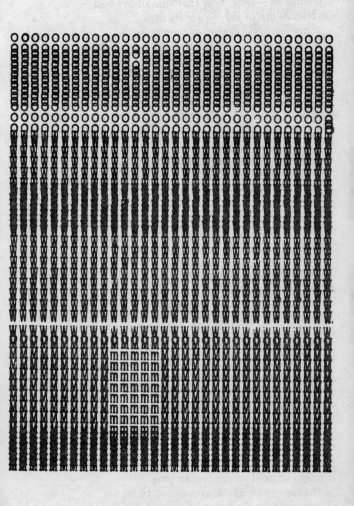

Killer Whale

". . . i want to tell you love . . ."
    —Milton Acorn

we were tryin to get back to Vancouver
again cumming down th sunshine coast,away
speeding from th power intrigue of a
desolate town,Powell River, feudalizd
totally by MacMillan Blowdell, a different
trip than when i was hitch-hiking back
once before with a cat who usd to live
next door to Ringo Starr's grandmother
who still lives in th same Liverpool house
even tho Ringo offerd her a town house
in London, still shops at th same places
moves among th Liverpool streets
with th peopul, like she dusint want
to know, this cat told me

away from th robot stink there,
after th preliminary hearing,martina
and me and th hot sun, arguing
our way thru th raspberry bushes
onto a bus headin for Van, on th ferry
analyzing th hearing and th bust, how
th whole insane trip cuts at our life
giving us suspicions and knowledge
stead of innocence and th bus takes
off without us from th bloody B.C.
government ferry—i can't walk too good
with a hole in my ankle and all why
we didn't stay with our friends back
at th farm—destind for more places
changes to go thru can feel th pull
of that heavy in our hearts and in th air,
th government workmen can't drive us
20 minutes to catch up with th bus, insane
complications,phoning Loffmark works minister

in Victoria capital if he sz so they will they say
he once wrote a fan letter to me on an
anti-Vietnam pome published in Prism," . . . with
interest . . ." he sd he red it, can't get him
on th phone, workmen say yer lucky if th
phone works, o lets dissolve all these phone
booths dotting surrealy our incognito intrigue
North American vast space, only cutting us all
off from each other—more crap with th bus
company, 2 hrs later nother ferry, hitch
ride groovy salesman of plastic bags, may
be weul work together we all laughing say
in th speeding convertibel to Garden City, he
wants to see there the captive killer whales.

Down past th town along th fishing boat dock
th killer whales, like Haida argolite carvings,
th sheen—black glistening, perfect white circuls
on th sides of them, th mother won't feed
th baby, protests her captivity, why did they
cum into this treacherous harbor, th times
without any challenge, for food, no food
out there old timer tells me, and caught,
millions of bait surrounding them, part of
th system, rather be food for th despondent
killer whales than be eat by th fattend ducks
on th shore there old timer tells me, and
if th baby dies no fault of mine th man
hosing him down strappd in a canvas sack
so he won't sink to th bottom, ive been hosing
him down 24 hrs a day since we netted em,
and out further a ways more killer whales
came in to see what was happening and they
got capturd for their concern, th cow howling
, thrashing herself in and out of th water, how
like i felt after getting busted, like we all
felt, yeah, th hosing down man told me, we got
enuff killer whales for 2 maybe 3 museums, course
th baby may die but there's still plenty for those

peopul whos never see animals like these
here lessen they went to a museum.

We went back to th convertible along th narrow
plank, heard th cow howl sum more, th bull
submergd, th man hosing th listless baby,
th sun's shattering light, them mammals aren't going
to take it lying down we thot, missed another ferry
connection, changd, made it, staggerd
together into town.

EVOLUTION OF LETTERS CHART

Old Greek	Euboean	Latin	Roman	Uncial	Miniscule		Venetian
A	A	A	A	A	a	a	a
B	B	B	B	B			b
Γ	Γ	<C C	C	C			c
		G	G				gg
Δ	D	D	D				d
E	E	E					
F	F	F					
I	I						
B	H	H					
Ʂ	I						
K	K	K					
V	L	LL	L	L			
M	M	M	M	m			
N	N	N	N	N			
Ŧ	+	X	X	X			
O	O	O	O				
Γ	Γ	PP	P	P			
Φ	Q	Q	Q				
D	R	RR	R				r
Σ	S	SS	S				s
T	T	T	T				t
Y	VY	UV	UV		w		uvw
		Y				y	y

"He told Quatta to stop" (p. 108)

bissett/69

...wer only human too were

what can we say what can we say what can we
what can we say what can we say what can we

keep yr cell clen

dirtyconcretepoet cobcretepoetcobcreteth
concrete dirty trty sum concrete sum

dirtdirtdirtdirtdirtdirtdirtdirtdirtdirtdirtdirtdirtdirtdirtdirt
dirtdirtdirtdirtdirtdirtdirtdirtdirtdirtdirtdirtdirtdirtdirtdirt
dddtdddtdddtdddtdtddtddtddtdtdtddtddtddtddtddtddtdtdtdtdtdtdt

a pome in praise of all quebec bombers

th tomato conspiracy aint
worth a whol pome

very few peopul
realize ths but altho yu have 5 or 6
billyun peopul walking around beleeving

that tomatoez ar red they ar
actually blu   nd ar sprayd
red to make ther apperance
consistent with peopuls beleef

i was whuns inside th
largest tomato spraying plant
in th world with binoculars nd
camoflage material all ovr me

nd ive got th pictures to proov it
oranges uv corz ar not orange nor ar lemons
lemon color   its all a mirage it

was decreed what color things
wud b at th beginning nd thn
theyve bin colord that
way evr since

it adds to th
chemicals nd artifishulness uv evrything
we eet tho did yu know that oranges
ar actually a discouraging off
color

i was luky really to get
out uv th tomato factoree alive
th tomatoez wer really
upset to b xposd

w h o s   o u t   t o n i t e

spring 78
bc transit informasyun

incident
a compleetly
strange
to me prson iud
nevr seen her bfor   sitting in
front uv me on th bus bags uv

grocerees in her arms   from

health food stores

startid yelling at me

aftr she askd
what kind uv paintings i mostly dew

fantasees part peopul part bird creatures i sd
sumtimes jumping sumtimes flying sumtimes astral
travelling nd with auras round ther hed
n wings for arms   with th sky nd
moon or sun n hills sumtimes
lifting ovr
ar they nudes she askd
i gess i sd
thats pornographee she sd
NUDES ARE BAD   ium thinking heer wer having a
conservativ backlash without evr having had
any revolusyun   she sd i shud paint hevn
nd what they want me to   i sd ths is
hevn   nudes ar peopul nd i paint
what i want to what th spirit
uv th painting is thru me

thats what an

artist duz

THERS NO NUDES ON TH SISTINE CHAPEL
she sd

look closr i sd
if yu wud paint what
they want yu to yu wudint b in debt she sd   thats
ok i sd   GET HEALTHY   she sd
i just had a check
up a yeer ago i sd   what dew yu want

OHHH she sd fuming   see yu latr i sd

i stayd on th bus til 3 stops aftr she got off

i did in anothr part uv paradise

PATRICK LANE

b. 1939

Loving She Stood Apart

loving she stood apart
and looked at me wanting
her and afraid she was
of the wanting to need
me watching her from
where I lay on the bed
as she undressed

and turned her back
to me undressed her
back was smooth the
angle of her hip so
I could touch her
holding my hand beside me
feet from where she was
her hands soft fingers
reaching out to me
from where they rested
on her shoulders afraid
to turn around and see me
see her eyes

turn out the light

she said and when I
made no move to move
my eyes to blackness
and the loss she said

please . . .

so quietly my mind
shut out the sight
and I was blind to
her but O the night

Elephants

The cracked cedar bunkhouse
hangs behind me like a grey pueblo
in the sundown where I sit
to carve an elephant
from a hunk of brown soap
for the Indian boy who lives
in the village a mile back
in the bush.

The alcoholic truck-driver
and the cat-skinner sit beside me
with their eyes closed
all of us waiting out the last hour
until we go back on the grade

and I try to forget the forever
clank   clank   clank
across the grade
pounding stones and earth to powder
for hours in mosquito darkness
of the endless cold mountain night.

The elephant takes form—
my knife caresses smooth soap
scaling off curls of brown
which the boy saves to take home
to his mother in the village

Finished, I hand the carving to him
and he looks at the image of the great
beast for a long time
then sets it on dry cedar
and looks up at me:

                  What's an elephant?

he asks
so I tell him of the elephants
and their jungles. The story
of the elephant graveyard
which no one has ever found
and how the silent
animals of the rain forest
go away to die somewhere
in the limberlost of distances
and he smiles

tells me of his father's
graveyard where his people have been
buried for years. So far back
no one remembers when it started
and I ask him where the graveyard is
and he tells me it is gone
now where no one will ever find it
buried under the grade of the new
highway.

Wild Horses

Just to come once alone
to these wild horses
driving out of the high Rockies
raw legs heaving the hip-high snow.
Just once alone. Never to see
the men and their trucks.

Just once alone. Nothing moves
as the stallion with five free mares
rush into the guns. All dead.
Their eyes glaze with frost.
Ice bleeds in their nostrils
as the cable hauls them in.

Later, after the swearing
and the stamping of feet
we ride down into Golden:

*Quit bitchin.
It's a hard bloody life
and a long week
for three hundred bucks of meat.*

That and the dull dead eyes
and the empty meadows.

Mountain Oysters

Kneeling in the sheep-shit
he picked up the biggest of the new rams
brushed the tail aside
slit the bag
tucked the knackers in his mouth
and clipped the cords off clean

the ram   stiff
with a single wild scream

as the tar went on
and he spit the balls in a bowl.

That's how we used to do it
when I was a boy.

It's no more gawdam painful
than any other way
and you can't have rams fighting
slamming it up every nanny

and enjoyed them with him
cutting delicately
into the deep-fried testicles.

Mountain oysters make you strong

he said
while out in the field
the rams stood holding their pain
legs fluttering like blue hands
of old tired men.

At the Edge of the Jungle

At the edge of the jungle
I watch a dog bury his head
in the mud of the Amazon
to drive away the hovering
mass of flies around his eyes.
The swarm expands like a lung
and settles again on the wound.

I turn to where orchids gape
like the vulvas of hanged women.
Everything is a madness:
a broken melon bleeds a pestilence
of bees; a woman squats and pees
balancing perfectly her basket
of meat; a gelding falls to its knees
under the goad of its driver.

interesting note:
- have twisted
ovary
from Greek
orchis -
testicle
from shape
of Roots

Images catch at my skull like thorns.
I no longer believe
the sight I have been given
and live inside the eyes of a rooster
who walks around a pile of broken bones.
Children have cut away his beak
and with a string have staked him
where he sees but cannot eat.

Diseased clouds bloom in the sky.
They throw down roots of fire.
The bird drags sound from its skin.
I am grown older than I imagined:
the garden I dreamed does not exist
and compassion is only the beginning
of suffering. Everything deceives.

A man could walk into this jungle
and lying down be lost
among the green sucking of trees.
What reality there is resides
in the child who holds the string
and does not see
the bird as it beats its blunt head
again and again into the earth.

Thirty Below

Men on the pond
push logs through constant ice.
Faces stubble with frost.
No one moves beyond the ritual
of work. Torment of metal
and the scream of saws.

Everything is hard. The sky
scrapes the earth at thirty below
and living things pull into pain
like grotesque children
thrown in the wrong season.

Someone curses.
Pulls his hand from the chain.
His skin has been left on steel,
blood frozen into balls.
He is replaced and the work goes on.

Everything is hard.
Cold lances the slow dance
on the pond. The new man trembles
out of control.
He can't hold his pole.
Someone laughs,
says it will be breakup
before they shut this damn mill down.

I Am Tired of Your Politics

'BE POLITICAL, IMPERSONAL WITH PASSION'
Dorothy Livesay

Let us remove our vanities
bring our dreams and end
even this with an embrace.
The bitch is old. She sleeps
in the sun with her head
heavy on her paws. The birds
conclude that noise
is an uncertain violence.
We must not hide
our innocence, the distant
singing we call love.

Lady, I am baffled
by your care. The mind is
always a dull thunder.
Shall we make politics
out of love? The bitch
is old. She sleeps in the sun,
decently, with a gift
for silence.

Shall we sing other than
our lives? Peace, wisdom,
excellence in the small
affairs of the heart?
But it is not only an old dog
we speak of nor the quiet
of the birds who grace
her age with their flight.

Listen, once when I was
young, I knew a woman
natural as beauty, brave
with all the mysteries
she was born to.
Let us not pity her.
The sad compassions
are of little use.
She left her love
in a thousand beds
until she lost her mind
and fell into the
dream called death.

Let us respect her now,
give her at least the desire
that she could be in the sun
with her hurt head resting
on her pale white hands.
The will is not holy.
One moves in stillness.
Look, even the birds
are decently silent
while she sleeps.

DENNIS LEE

b. 1939

400: Coming Home

You are still on the highway and the great light of
noon comes over the asphalt, the gravelled
shoulders. You are on the highway, there is a kind of
laughter, the cars pound
south. Over your shoulder the scrub-grass, the fences,
the fields wait patiently as though someone
believed in them. The light has laid it
upon them. One
crow scrawks. The edges
take care of themselves, there is
no strain, you can almost hear it, you
inhabit it.

Back in the city many things you lived for
are coming apart.
Transistor rock still fills
back yards, in the parks young men do things to
hondas; there will be
heat lightning, beer on the porches, goings on.
That is not it.

And you are still on the highway. There are no
houses, no farms. Across the median, past the swish and
      thud of the
northbound cars, beyond the opposite
fences, the fields, the
climbing escarpment, solitary in the
bright eye of the sun the
birches dance, and they
dance. They have

their reasons. You do not know
anything.
Cicadas call now, in the darkening swollen air there is dust
in your nostrils; a
kind of laughter; you are still on the highway.

1838

The Compact sat in parliament
To legalize their fun.
And now they're hanging Sammy Lount
And Captain Anderson.
And if they catch Mackenzie
They will string him in the rain.
And England will erase us if
Mackenzie comes again.

The Bishop has a paper
That says he owns our land.
The Bishop has a Bible too
That says our souls are damned.
Mackenzie had a printing press.
It's soaking in the Bay.
And who will spike the Bishop till
Mackenzie comes again?

The British want the country
For the Empire and the view.
The Yankees want the country for
A yankee barbecue.
The Compact want the country
For their merrie green domain.
They'll all play finder's-keepers till
Mackenzie comes again.

Mackenzie was a crazy man.
He wore his wig askew.
He donned three bulky overcoats
In case the bullets flew.
Mackenzie talked of fighting
While the fight went down the drain.
But who will speak for Canada?
Mackenzie, come again!

Thursday

Powerful men can fuck up too. It is Thursday,
a mean old lady has died, she got him his
paper route and there is still that whiff of
ju-jube and doilies from her front hall; a stroke; he can
taste them going soggy; some in his pocket too, they always
    picked up
lint; anyway, she is dead.
And tonight there are things to do in the study, he has a
report, he has the kids, it is
almost too much. Forty-five years, and
still the point eludes him whenever he stops to think.
Next morning,
hacking the day into shape on the phone, there is still no
way—routine & the small ache,
he cannot accommodate both.
At Hallowe'en too, in her hall.
And I know which one he takes and that
night at six, while the kids are tackling his legs with their
    small tussling,
how he fends them off, tells them "Play upstairs"; one day
they will be dead also with their jelly beans.
In her kitchen, she had a parrot that said "Down the hatch!"

FROM *Civil Elegies*

2

Master and Lord, where
are you?
A man moves back and forth
between what must be done to save the world
and what will save his soul,
and neither is real. For many years
I could not speak your name, nor now but
even stilled at times by openings like
joy my whole life
aches, the streets I walk along to work declare
your absence, the headlines
declare it, the nation, and
over and over the harried lives I
watch and live with, holding my breath and
sometimes a thing rings true—
they all give way and declare your real absence.

Master and Lord,
let be, I can say
nothing about you that does not
vanish like tapwater.
I know
the world is not enough; a woman straightens
and turns from the sink and asks her life the
question, why should she
fake it? and after a moment she
shrugs, and returns to the sink. A man's
adrenalin takes hold, at a meeting he makes
his point, and pushes and sees that
things will happen now . . . and then in the pause he knows
there are endless things in the world and this is not for real.

Whatever is lovely, whatever deserves
contempt, whatever dies—
over and over, in every thing we meet
we meet that emptiness.

It is a homecoming, as men once knew
their lives took place in you.
And we cannot get on, no matter how we
rearrange our lives and we cannot let go for
then there is nothing at all.

Master and Lord, there was a
measure once.
There was a time when men could say
my life, my job, my home
and still feel clean.
The poets spoke of earth and heaven. There were no symbols.

9

Here, as I sit and watch, the rusty leaves hang taut with
      departure.
The last few tourists pose by the Moore and snap their proof
      that they were also alive.
And what if there is no regenerative absence?
What if the void that compels us is only
a mood gone absolute?
We would have to live in the world.
What if the dreary high-rise is nothing but
banks of dreary high-rise, it does not
release the spirit by fraying its attachment,
for the excellent reason that there is no place else to go?
We would have to live in it, making our lives on earth.
Or else a man might go on day by day
in love with emptiness, dismayed each time he meets
good friends, fine buildings and grass in the acres of
      concrete, feeling the
city's erotic tug begin once more, perpetually
splayed alive by the play of his bungled desires,
though some do not salute the death of the body
before they have tested its life, but crippled they summon
      together
the fury from within, they tilt at
empire, empire, lethal adversary;

but I am one who came to
idolatry, as in a season of God,
taking my right to be from nothingness.

Across the square the crisp leaves blow in gusts, tracing
the wind's indignant lift in corners,
filling the empty pool.
People plod past through the raw air, lost in their overcoats.
I hunch down close to my chest and eat smoke.

But when the void became void I did
let go, though derelict for months
and I was easy, no longer held by its negative presence
as I was earlier disabused of many things in the world
including Canada, and came to know I still had access to
        them,
and I promised to honour each one of my country's failures
        of nerve and its sellouts.

To rail and flail at a dying civilisation,
to rage in imperial space, condemning
soviet bombers, american bombers—to go on saying
no to history is good.
And yet a man does well to leave that game behind, and go
        and find
some saner version of integrity,
although he will not reach it where he longs to, in the
vacant spaces of his mind—they are so
occupied. Better however to try.

But we are not allowed to enter God's heaven, where it is all a
drowsy beatitude, nor is God, the realm above our heads but
must grow up on earth.
Nor do we have recourse to void.
For void is not a place, nor
negation of a place.
Void is not the high cessation of the lone self's burden,
crowned with the early nostalgias;
nor is it rampant around the corner, endlessly possible.
We enter void when void no longer exists.

And best of all is finding a place to be
in the early years of a better civilisation.
For we are a conquered nation: sea to sea we bartered
everything that counts, till we have
nothing to lose but our forebears' will to lose.
Beautiful riddance!
And some will make their choice and eat imperial meat.
But many will come to themselves, for there is
no third way at last and these will
spend their lives at war, though not with
guns, not yet—with motherwit and guts, sustained
by bloody-minded reverence among the things which are,
and the long will to be in Canada.

The leaves, although they cling against the
wind do not resist their time of dying.
And I must learn to live it all again, depart again—
the storm-wracked crossing, the nervous descent, the barren
        wintry land,
and clearing a life in the place where I belong, re-entry
to bare familiar streets, first sight of coffee mugs,
reconnaissance of trees, of jobs done well or badly,
flashes of workday people abusing their power,
abusing their lives, hung up, sold out and
feeling their lives wrenched out of whack
by the steady brunt of the continental breakdown;
finding a place among the ones who live
on earth somehow, sustained in fits and starts
by the deep ache and presence and sometimes the joy of
        what is.

Freely out of its dignity the void must
supplant itself. Like God like the soul it must
surrender its ownness, like eternity it must
re-instil itself in the texture of our being here.
And though we have seen our most precious words
withdraw, like smudges of wind from a widening water-calm,
though they will not be charged with presence again in our
        lifetime that is

as well, for now we have access to new nouns—
as water, copout, tower, body, land.

Earth, you nearest, allow me.
Green of the earth and civil grey:
within me, without me and moment by
moment allow me for to
be here is enough and earth you
strangest, you nearest, be home.

The Gods

I

Who, now, can speak of gods—
their strokes and carnal voltage,
old ripples of presence   a space ago
archaic eddies of being?

Perhaps a saint could speak their names.
Or maybe some
noble claustrophobic spirit,
crazed by the flash and
vacuum of modernity,
could reach back, ripe for
gods and a hot lobotomy.
But being none of these, I sit
bemused by the sound of the words.
For a man no longer moves
through coiled ejaculations of
meaning;
we dwell within
taxonomies, equations, paradigms
which deaden the world and now in our
heads, though less in our inconsistent lives,
the tickle of cosmos is gone.

Though what would a god be *like*—
                    would he shop at Dominion?
Would he know about DNA molecules? and keep little
        haloes, for when they behaved?
                    ... It is not from simple derision
        that the imagination snickers. But faced with an alien
                    reality it
        stammers, it races & churns
                    for want of a common syntax and
                        lacking a possible language
        who, now, can speak of gods? for random example
                    a bear to our forebears, and even to
grope in a pristine hunch back to that way of being on earth
                    is nearly beyond me.

                                II

                            And yet—
in the middle of one more day, in a clearing maybe   sheer
                            godforce
            calm on the lope of its pads
        furred   hot-breathing   erect, at ease, catastrophic
                    harsh waves of stink, the
            dense air clogged with its roaring and
                ripples of power fork through us:
        hair gone electric quick
                    pricklish glissando, the
        .   skin   mind skidding, balking is
                        HAIL
and it rears foursquare and we are jerked and owned and
                            forgive us   and
                brought to a welter, old
            force & destroyer and
                            do not destroy us!
                    or if it seems good,
                        destroy us.

Thus, the god against us in clear air.
        And there are gentle gods—
             as plain as
          light that
             rises from lake-face,
      melding with light
that skips like a stepping-stone spatter
           down to
                evoke it
till blue embraces blue, and lake and sky
           are miles of indigenous climax—
    such grace in the shining air.

    All gods, all gods and none of them
             domesticated angels, chic of spat & wing
    on ten-day tours of earth. And if
to speak of 'gods' recalls those antique
           wind-up toys, forget the gods as well:
             tremendum rather,
dimension of otherness, come clear
        in each familiar thing—in
outcrop, harvest, hammer, beast and
           caught in that web of otherness
        we too endure & we
        worship.
Men lived among that force, a space ago.

        Or,
whirling it reins into phase through us, good god it can
      use us, power in tangible
    dollops invading the roots of the
    hair, the gap behind the neck,
power to snag, coax bully exalt into presence
    clean gestures of meaning among
    the traffic of earth,

and until it lobs us aside, pale snot poor
             rags we
        also can channel the godforce.
                                 Yet still ne
   abject: not
          heaven & wistful hankering—I mean
       the living power, inside
                and, that sudden that
          plumb!
          Men lived in such a space.

III

   I do say gods.
  But that was time ago, technology
              happened and what has been withdrawn
   I do not understand, the absent ones,
though many then too were bright & malevolent and
             crushed things that mattered,
and where they have since been loitering I scarcely
             comprehend,
    and least of all can I fathom, you powers I
   seek and no doubt cheaply arouse and
       who are you?
how I am to salute you, nor how contend with your being
for I do not aim to make prize-hungry words (and stay back!

I want
the world to be real and
it will not,
for to secular men there is not given the glory of tongues,
yet it is
better to speak in silence than squeak in the gab of the age
and if I cannot tell your terrifying
praise, now Hallmark gabble and chintz nor least of all
what time and dimensions your naked incursions
announced, you scurrilous powers yet
still I stand against this bitch of a shrunken time
in semi-faithfulness
and whether you are godhead or zilch or daily ones like before
you strike our measure still and still you
endure as my murderous fate,
though I
do not know you.

Remember, Woman

Remember, woman, how we lay
Beside ourselves the livelong day
And tuned out all that heady fuss
And felt new lives invading us?

We loved, as though our bodies meant
To fire their own enlightenment,
And raise, despite our moral dread,
A carnal OM on a rumpled bed.

Remember how the light that shone
Spilled from within you? Off and on
The switch was easy; and we lit
Eternal brightness for a bit;

And me, I was so tightly strung
I could have pulled myself and rung,
Or pealed out gratis from the glans
A paradise for puritans.

Brothers, lovers, mothers, wives—
Glad ambush by a dozen lives.
Fresh selves of you, new many me,
A sacrament of letting be.

And loved on, in a bell-jar hush—
Ankle, breast and burning bush
The flesh was common, and we strayed
Ecstatic in our own parade.

Cocky beatitude! which sank
To getting by in brain and flank.
The fire went out; our lives grew sane.
Sweet Christ, I long for then again!

Summer Song

The light was free and easy then,
Among the maple trees,
And music drifted over
From the neighbours' balconies;
Half my mind was nodding
With the asters in their ranks,
And half was full to bursting
With a hungry kind of thanks.

It wasn't just the mottled play
Of light along the lawn.
I didn't hope to live back all the
Good times that were gone;
All I wanted was to let
The light and maples be,
Yet something came together as they
Entered into me.

And what was singing in my mind
Was in my body too:
Sun and lawn and aster beds
Murmuring, *I do* —
Earth, beloved, yes, I do I
Too am here by grace,
As real as any buried stone
Or any blade of grass.

Breath and death and pestilence
Were not revoked by that.
Heavy things went on, among
The calm magnificat.
Yet as I sat, my body spoke
The words of my return:
There is a joy of being, which you
Must be still and learn.

GWENDOLYN MACEWEN

b. 1941

Eden, Eden

the thunder is
a vocal monument
to the dying rain
or an obelisk in a granite sky
which roars an epitaph
through cut clouds.

in the morning
thunder is a reared stone elephant,
                              a grown element of grey;
its trunk is vertical and thick as—thunder;
it roars down the wrenched lightning
coughing out a verse
for the suicidal rain
in the morning.

the stormed man is heavy with rain
and mumbles beneath the elephant's gargle
and his jaws lock human in the rain,
and under the unlocked jaws of the split sky
and under the bullets of the elephant's trunk

he is thinking of a thunder garden.

behind sense he is thinking of a warped tree
with heavy fruit falling,
peaked rock fighting the ragged fern
in *another* storm-centre—
a monolithic thunder tree
and a man and woman naked and green with rain
above its carved roots, genesis

Poems in Braille

1

all your hands are verbs,
now you touch worlds and feel their names—
thru the thing to the name
not the other way thru (in winter
I am Midas, I name gold)

the chair and table and book
extend from your fingers;
all your movements
command these things back to their
places; a fight against familiarity
makes me resume my distance

2

they knew what it meant,
those egyptian scribes who drew
eyes right into their hieroglyphs,
you read them dispassionate until
the eye stumbles upon itself
blinking back from the papyrus

outside, the articulate wind
annotates this; I read carefully
lest I go blind in both eyes, reading with
that other eye the final hieroglyph

3

the shortest distance between 2 points
on a revolving circumference
is a curved line; O let me follow you,
Wenceslas

4

with legs and arms I make alphabets
like in those children's books
where people bend into letters and signs,
yet I do not read the long cabbala of my bones
truthfully; I need only to move
to alter the design

5

I name all things in my room
and they rehearse their names,
gather in groups, form tesseracts,
discussing their names among themselves

I will not say the cast is less than the print
I will not say the curve is longer than the line,
I should read all things like braille in this season
with my fingers I should read them
lest I go blind in both eyes reading with
that other eye the final hieroglyph

The Caravan

precede me into this elusive country,
travel the tracks of my old laughter,
tame this landscape, and I will follow after—
yet do not let this desert inherit you,
absorb your caravan into sand—
(which is your body, which is the land?)
O love elude me, this recurring journey
darkens my speech, disorients me
forever from my natural country,
while the orient eye decides geography.

bandar abbes, el minya, el gatrun,
taif, dongola, beni abbes . . .
(once, during an eclipse
the polarities of my body argued me out
from an arctic dream
and I journeyed east, and south,
to enter the final africa of your mouth)

my caravan falters, stops and starts,
its tracks upon the sand are arabesque;
this night is a dream of jackals
and disorient, I cannot decide which turn is best,
and so I circle, so I dance—
(precede me into this elusive country)
always this place, this latitude escapes me

The Shadow-Maker

I have come to possess your darkness, only this.

My legs surround your black, wrestle it
As the flames of day wrestle night
And everywhere you paint the necessary shadows
On my flesh and darken the fibres of my nerve;
Without these shadows I would be
In air one wave of ruinous light
And night with many mouths would close
Around my infinite and sterile curve.

Shadow-maker create me everywhere
Dark spaces (your face is my chosen abyss),
For I said I have come to possess your darkness,
Only this.

The Armies of the Moon

now they begin to gather their forces
in the Marsh of Decay and the Sea of Crises;
their leaders stand motionless
on the rims of the craters
invisible and silver as swords turned sideways
waiting for earthrise and the coming of man.

they have always been there increasing their numbers
at the foot of dim rills, all around and under
the ghostly edges where moonmaps surrender
and hold out white flags to the night.

when the earthmen came hunting with wagons and golfballs
they were so eager for white rocks and sand
that they did not see them, invisible and silver
as swords turned sideways on the edge of the craters—
so the leaders assumed they were blind.

in the Lake of Death there will be a showdown;
men will be powder, they will go down under
the swords of the unseen silver armies,
become one with the gorgeous anonymous moon.

none of us will know what caused the crisis
as the lunar soldiers reluctantly disband
and return to their homes in the Lake of Dreams
weeping quicksilver tears for the blindness of man.

As the Angels

As the angels and the animals lie
As the saints and leopards sleep
In a huge heap in some forgotten corner
Of the universe
So shall I sleep, O so shall I

Meanwhile I watch as man, O man
That hairless hunter, that gutless wonder
Rides by night in the dark night air
With his floating kidneys
And his ears on fire

I have many secrets
And no particular future

I am surreal and finally here

I am a perfect animal

As the angels and the animals lie
As the saints and leopards go to sleep
So then, so then shall I

Tall Tales

It has been said that I sometimes lie, or bend the truth
        to suit me. Did I make that four hundred mile
        trip alone in Turkish territory or not?
        I wonder if it is anybody's business
        to know. Syria is still there,
        and the long lie that the war was.

Was there a poster of me offering money for my capture,
        and did I stand there staring at myself,
        daring anyone to know me? Consider
        truth and untruth, consider why they call them
        the *theatres* of war. All of us
        played our roles to the hilt.

Poets only play with words, you know; they too
        are masters of the Lie, the Grand Fiction.
        Poets and men like me who fight for something
        contained in words, but not words.

What if the whole show was a lie, and it bloody well was—
        would I still lie to you? Of course I would.

DAPHNE MARLATT

b. 1942 "parents from England.

for k, d

sun finds you two
curved

shells on our bed
in a deep
white you're tide
carved

only the
hull of your push.

"sculptural energy is the mountain"

GAUDIER-BRZESKA

for satis
faction face flat blind
sun she
rubs to mine the feel of
small fur her sheer
joy

standby/

scarcely e
nuf of touch the
suns's mechanics as the
tower did rise

gaudy a
rodia flesh
hulled pebbles &
other small
articles of faith the
tower did rise

tangere
noli me tangere or
snow the way she
walks off.

so cocksure

i

momentum

eventually of stars
runs down
hill,
    the shingle

back't us slippery
feet collide with dry
sky

ii

as simply
spoken out as even
its tongue
licks lights lightens its
hunger hole in
visible over

black water, branches

lie under
lined our
laughter his
half-expected
emergence from

(handwritten: — a moon?
her Man?)

iii

warm to
touch

iv

unspoken his
head of
stars stares
a head

that lie that eyes
suffice

that we shd kiss & make
up he sd before
driving to
sleep.

(handwritten, vertical/diagonal: Ling. tension of potential meaning no subject no predicate just a moment of meaning)

At Birch Bay

FOR ROY
(thanks to Charles Olson)

(handwritten: — Black Mountain Poet)

black, crow, leap up   fall, flap nervous wings against a steep
invisible.   bank,   against wind flutters, settle,   has none
    of the
sweep & glide these gulls have   open to this incessant,
oncoming tide   waves & foam   wind

(handwritten: The Raven — poe)

(handwritten: — 4 line Stanza)
(handwritten: — ghestola structure)
(handwritten: — Subject: black crow)

Crow, rise &
(drop something   rise & (drop,   flutter,   in to his own
    stress
landing against this wind, over & over. Cracking shells,
    having
learned this from the gulls?

                thru time, in the rising
wind last night I dreamt, & see, now, like the crow
    what it is I
learn from you
              walking
                    walking the night as moon, moves
cancer, out of sea & moon pre-eminent, walking the long.
    tiderow-
beach. alone: white shells, white backs of gulls on the
    further
strand,   lift,   onto the air, clapping wings at their
re-entry into the element,   birds,   know wind changes
fast as the moon, how tide makes sand disappear, no place
    to be
except the turbulent face of sea itself incessant. . .

                        It was you
                        who
entered my dream, entered me,   in the rising wind last
    night, in love
in the wash of opening seas we come together in: something
    about a
newborn you saw (rise & drop, rise &) drop   a long life
    line down
thru all these threshing seas, these birds, like refugees, are
    resting in
cloud earth sky sensorium   outside my dream, outside our
    dream—"ends &
boundaries," or "'space-activities' in, Creation." Within
    which, this
marvellous "Animate" you teach me, along with the sweep
    & glide these
gulls possess   this (shell) their & our   one & only   world.

4/75

Constellation

(WATTS, NEWARK, DETROIT . . .)

Lady
bug lady
running
up table, sky's
aflame your
children are gone

    homeless, the
    song goes
    home
        does not, we

inhabit sky
one foot
    (herculean
on earth which
tables her, she
nervous shakes
quick wings, wait!

the two parts of
your song,
        Night
coming on

my son with milk
satiate
in temporary arms all
children claim
    fearless for
however long—
        This Night
        Children Burn

blocks &
blocks changing
rockets
home made bomb bursts
nerve system clusters
light in
          /corporate

Lady bug
mother of
flame you
cannot fly

milk & the starry
nipple nebulae we
all desire

          connect

us in our rights, to
this once & only home
we go on burning

light writes

in & out your window, woman with the trees in your face,
          with the sea,
fed by the mountains you said, not by the city, burning,
          frames the   /
people of this city walk through, out your window into
          what looks
out at what looks back, is caught up, catches, light inside
          their
black slow fire i'm eaten up, i'm burning, you a flesh or
          dreaming
i am not, a tongue to lick alight the dark your images
          project,
eyes looking out of darkness in that head. . .

2/79

New Moon

FOR ROY

A windowpane fingernail moon last night, coming into the
    dark room for something
outside light, where I'd left him   in the bath   having clipt
    tiny fingernails all
over the blue carpet—all over the blue so black stars shine
    moon mostly a
finger of light appears at the crack of the door, dark, dark,
    circle a child
sits arm around knees—listens to their voices in the other
    room, promise
time holds, or light (see to the full like some pencil mark in
    the night sky
so faint it is the reverse of night) imagining the other side of
    where he sits
hugging himself in a shoe or moon, in a funny clog he sails
    off in, wishing. . .

briars, wishing a gate, a way *into* what remains dark for
    you, the
nave of an abandoned church like the belly of some whale
    you call me on the
phone in full daylight full of the excitement of.   This is a
    ship beached in
quiet halfway up a hill overlooking the sea.   This is the
    architrave of
sleep, "reaching 25 feet up," into invisible light on the
    other side of dream.
"I've found the place I want to live in"
                (briar rose)
                    & does it sleep
at night on an empty road? do you? Nothing sleeps, not
    even that briar which buds
inside you, waiting spellbound for the door to open, your
    door, your hand on it.

Here, I have just finished planting beans & marigolds, those
    flowers of the sun.
New moon, our neighbour said, I been waiting all month for
    this, new moon & moon
in taurus, figure you can't get more earthy than that. Here
    is an architecture
of gardens, a block whose visible fences hide, under the
    night, the invisible
sympathy of seeds & moon. The same you, across a sea,
    wake under, walk in my
imagining that white expanse of beach, dark ribs, white
    whale or white reflected
walls this moon a door we can't afford to look at, opens, in
    reverse, onto a
brilliant terrain love lives inside of, dwarfed by a rising
    earth, its changes.

5/75

seeing your world from the outside

                         outside night, light
absence is whirling down.   down the order of night,   not
    upside,   out—
alleyways, all ways the walls say no.

                       standing inside your world
                           is
full of holes   floating   doors: "a scream is an
    appraisal."   you.
apprised of what we see are messages off walls.

                         & let me read
the black tint under your eyes from banging your head
    all night, against
the wall of your own want. "salud! ladies of the
    night."   who do not
win *(Express yourself)*

             Do Not Phone. Do Not move on to Go.

this game is rigged. because somebody has to be at the
    bottom, lottery system,
lots have to be at the bottom so somebody else comes out
    on top.   because
everybody wants.   & chance is the midnight bus with the
    winning number: will it
stop where you stop? is this the right spot? is this a stop
    at all?   stop.

the night is full of losers & empty buses, palisades of light
    adrift. nosed in
to the curb, some slight collision, lights still on, sits under
    neon, nothing
left to lose.   black are the scrawls of want on the walls that
    do not see us
("annie was here") to be lost ("take me home") in want,
    o baby, "will you still
feed me? will you still need me?"

black & white. & you. standing inside your world are
    photographing doors or
holes in the wall night pours thru.   "a scream is an
    appraisal."   you. a scream
is a refusal.   we.   refuse to keep in all that silence pressing
    thru the walls
o women, women who write

               "because the night belongs to us"

11/78

MICHAEL ONDAATJE

b. 1943

The Diverse Causes

*for than all erbys and treys renewyth a man and woman,
and in lyke wyse lovers callyth to their mynde olde
jantylnes and olde servyse, and many kynde dedes that
was forgotyn by neclygence*

Three clouds and a tree
reflect themselves on a toaster.
The kitchen window hangs scarred,
shattered by winter hunters.

We are in a cell of civilised magic.
Stravinsky roars at breakfast,
our milk is powdered.

Outside, a May god
moves his paws to alter wind
to scatter shadows of tree and cloud.
The minute birds walk confident
jostling the cold grass.
The world not yet of men.

We clean buckets of their sand
to fetch water in the morning,
reach for winter cobwebs,
sweep up moths who have forgotten to waken.
When the children sleep, angled
behind their bottles, you can hear mice prowl.

I turn a page
careful not to break the rhythms
of your sleeping head on my hip,
watch the moving under your eyelid
that turns like fire,
and we have love and the god outside
until the ice starts to limp
in brown hidden waterfalls,
or my daughter burns the lake
by reflecting her red shoes in it.

Henri Rousseau and Friends

FOR BILL MUYSSON

In his clean vegetation
the parrot, judicious,
poses on a branch.
The narrator of the scene,
aware of the perfect fruits,
the white and blue flowers,
the snake with an ear for music;
he presides.

The apes
hold their oranges like skulls,
like chalices.
They are below the parrot
above the oranges—
a jungle serfdom which
with this order
reposes.

They are the ideals of dreams.
Among the exactness,
the symmetrical petals,
the efficiently flying angels,
there is complete liberation.
The parrot is interchangeable;

tomorrow in its place
a waltzing man and tiger,
brash legs of a bird.

Greatness achieved
they loll among textbook flowers
and in this pose hang
scattered like pearls
in just as intense a society.
On Miss Adelaide Milton de Groot's walls,
with Lillie P. Bliss in New York.

And there too
in spangled wrists and elbows
and grand façades of cocktails
are vulgarly beautiful parrots, appalled lions,
the beautiful and the forceful locked in suns,
and the slight, careful stepping birds.

In Another Fashion

The cat performs,
rippling shoulder
on a strip of fence.
Pneumatic scratching
beats each jaw, shows
earrings of scar
through yellow leaves
and laundry.

We must build new myths
to wind up the world,
provoke new christs
with our beautiful women,
bring

plumed
thin boned birds
to claw carpets
to betray
majesty in a sway

Pale birds
with rings on ugly feet

to drink from clear bowls
to mate with our children

Peter

I

That spring Peter was discovered, freezing
the maze of bones from a dead cow,
skull and hooves glazed
with a skin of ice.
The warmth in his hands
carved hollows of muscle,
his fingers threading veins on its flank.

In the attempt to capture him
he bit, to defend himself,
three throats and a wrist;
that night villagers found the cow
frozen in red, and Peter
eating a meal beside it.

Ii

They snared him in evening light,
his body a pendulum
between the walls of the yard,
rearing from shrinking flashes of steel
until they, with a new science,

stretched his heels and limbs,
scarred through the back of his knees
leaving his veins unpinned,
and him singing in the evening air.

Till he fainted, and a brown bitch
nosed his pain, stared in interest,
and he froze into consciousness
to drag his feet to the fountain,
to numb wounds.

III

In the first months of his capture
words were growls, meaningless;
disgust in his tone burned everyone.
At meals, in bed, you heard Peter's howl
in the depths of the castle like a bell.
After the first year they cut out his tongue;

difficult
to unpin a fish's mouth
without the eventual jerk
to empty throat of pin and matter.

There followed months of silence,
then the eventual grunting;
he begain to speak with the air of his body,
torturing breath into tones; it was despicable,
they had made a dead animal of his throat.

He was little more than a marred stone,
a baited gargoyle, escaped
from the fountain in the courtyard:
his throat swollen like an arm muscle,
his walk stuttered with limp, his knees straight,
his feet arcing like a compass.

IV

They made a hive for him in the court,
Jason throwing him bones from the table,
the daughter Tara tousling in detail
the hair that collapsed like a nest
over his weaving eyes.
She, with bored innocence,
would pet him like a flower,
place vast kisses on his wrists,
thrilled at scowls and obscenities,
delighted at sudden grins
that opened his face like a dawn.

He ate, bouldered at their feet,
vast hands shaping rice,
and he walked with them on grit drives—
his legs dragged like a suitcase behind him.

V

All this while Peter formed violent beauty.
He carved death on chalices,
made spoons of yawning golden fishes;
forks stemmed from the tongues of reptiles,
candle holders bent like the ribs of men.

He made fragments of people: breasts
in the midst of a girl's stride,
a head burrowed in love,
an arm swimming—fingers heaved
to nose barricades of water.

His squat form, the rippled arms
of seaweeded hair,
the fingers black, bent from moulding silver,
poured all his strength
into the bare reflection of eyes

VI

Then Tara grew.

When he first saw her, tall,
ungainly as trees,
her fat knees dangled his shoulders
as her hips rode him,
the court monster, she
swaying from side to side, held
only by the grip of her thighs
on his obtuse neck —
she bending over him,
muttering giggles at his eyes,
covering his creased face with her hair.

And he made golden spiders for her
and silver frogs, with opal glares.

And as she grew, her body
burned its awkwardness.
The full bones roamed
in brown warm skin.
The ridge in her back broadened,
her dress hid seas of thighs,
arms trailed to adjust hair that paused
like a long bird at her shoulder;
and vast brown breasts
restless at each gesture
clung to her body like new sea beasts.

And she smiled cool at Peter now,
a quiet hand received gifts from him,
and her fingers, poised,
touched
to generate expressions.

VII

An arm held her, splayed
its fingers like a cross at her neck
till he could feel fear thrashing at her throat,
while his bent hands tore the sheet of skirt,
lifted her, buttock and neck to the table.
Then laying arm above her breasts
he shaped her body like a mould,
the stub of tongue sharp as a cat, cold,
dry as a cat, rasping neck and breasts
till he poured loathing of fifteen years on her,
a vat of lush oil, staining,
the large soft body like a whale.

Then he lay there breathing at her neck
his face wet from her tears
that glued him to her pain.

'The Gate in His Head'

FOR VICTOR COLEMAN

Victor, the shy mind
revealing the faint scars
coloured strata of the brain,
not clarity but the sense of shift

a few lines, the tracks of thought

Landscape of busted trees
the melted tires in the sun
Stan's fishbowl
with a book inside
turning its pages
like some sea animal
camouflaging itself
the typeface clarity
going slow blonde in the sun full water

My mind is pouring chaos
in nets onto the page.
A blind lover, dont know
what I love till I write it out.
And then from Gibson's your letter
with a blurred photograph of a gull.
Caught vision. The stunning white bird
an unclear stir.

And that is all this writing should be then.
The beautiful formed things caught at the wrong moment
so they are shapeless, awkward
moving to the clear.

King Kong Meets Wallace Stevens

Take two photographs—
Wallace Stevens and King Kong
(Is it significant that I eat bananas as I write this?)

Stevens is portly, benign, a white brush cut
striped tie. Businessman but
for the dark thick hands, the naked brain
the thought in him.

Kong is staggering
lost in New York streets again
a spawn of annoyed cars at his toes.
The mind is nowhere.
Fingers are plastic, electric under the skin.
He's at the call of Metro-Goldwyn-Mayer.

Meanwhile W. S. in his suit
is thinking chaos is thinking fences.
In his head—the seeds of fresh pain
his exorcising,
the bellow of locked blood.

The hands drain from his jacket,
pose in the murderer's shadow.

Published in "Rat Jelly" [handwritten annotation]

Spider Blues

"WELL I MADE THEM LAUGH, I WISH I COULD MAKE THEM CRY."
—David McFadden *Toronto Poet* [handwritten annotation]

My wife has a smell that spiders go for.
At night they descend saliva roads
down to her dreaming body.
They are magnetized by her breath's rhythm,
leave their own constructions
for succulent travel across her face and shoulder.
My own devious nightmares
are struck to death by her shrieks.

Self Reflexive writing about himself writing about poetry [handwritten annotation]

About the spiders.
Having once tried to play the piano
and unable to keep both hands
segregated in their intent
I admire the spider, his control classic,
his eight legs finicky,
making lines out of the juice in his abdomen.
A kind of writer I suppose.

literary meaning w/ narrative [handwritten annotation]

He thinks a path and travels
the emptiness that was there
leaves his bridge behind
looking back saying Jeez
did I do that?
and uses his ending
to swivel to new regions
where the raw of feelings exist.

Spiders like poets are obsessed with power.
They write their murderous art which sleeps
like stars in the corner of rooms,
a mouth to catch audiences
weak   broken   sick

writer as spider [handwritten annotation]

And spider comes to fly, says
Love me I can kill you, love me
my intelligence has run rings about you
love me, I kill you for the clarity that
comes when roads I make are being made
love me, antisocial, lovely.
And fly says, O no
no your analogies are slipping
no I choose who I die with
you spider poets are all the same
you in your close vanity of making,
you minor drag, your saliva stars always
soaking up the liquid from our atmosphere.
And the spider in his loathing
crucifies his victims in his spit
making them the art he cannot be.

So. The ending we must arrive at.
                        ok folks.

Nightmare for my wife and me:

It was a large white room
and the spiders had thrown
their scaffolds off the floor
onto four walls and the ceiling.
They had surpassed themselves this time
and with the white roads
their eight legs built with speed
they carried her up—her whole body
into the dreaming air so gently
she did not wake or scream.
What a scene. So many trails
the room was a shattered pane of glass.
Everybody clapped, all the flies.
They came and gasped,
everybody cried at the beauty
ALL
except the working black architects
and the lady locked in their dream   their theme

[handwritten annotations in margin:] These lines echo Purdy

Nebokov's *Ada* - spider has origins in this book ⤷ story about incest.

Plunging yourself into the forbidden pleasure of flesh

White Dwarfs

This is for people who disappear
for those who descend into the code
and make their room a fridge for Superman
—who exhaust costume and bones that could
        perform flight,
who shave their moral so raw
they can tear themselves through the eye of a needle
this is for those people
that hover and hover
and die in the ether peripheries

There is my fear
of no words   of
falling without words
over and over   of
mouthing the silence
Why do I love most
among my heroes those
who sail to that perfect edge
where there is no social fuel
Release of sandbags
to understand their altitude—

                that silence of the third cross
                3rd man hung so high and lonely
                we don't hear him say
                say his pain, say his unbrotherhood
                What has he to do with the smell of ladies
                can they eat off his skeleton of pain?

The Gurkhas in Malaya
cut the tongues of mules
so they were silent beasts of burden
in enemy territories
after such cruelty what could they speak of anyway
And Dashiell Hammett in success
suffered conversation and moved
to the perfect white between the words

This white that can grow
is fridge, bed,
is an egg—most beautiful
when unbroken, where
what we cannot see is growing
in all the colours we cannot see

there are those burned out stars
who implode into silence
after parading in the sky
after such choreography what would they wish to speak
    of   anyway

Letters & Other Worlds

"FOR THERE WAS NO MORE DARKNESS FOR HIM AND, NO DOUBT
LIKE ADAM BEFORE THE FALL, HE COULD SEE IN THE DARK"

> My father's body was a globe of fear
> His body was a town we never knew
> He hid that he had been where we were going
> His letters were a room he seldom lived in
> In them the logic of his love could grow
>
> My father's body was a town of fear
> He was the only witness to its fear dance
> He hid where he had been that we might lose him
> His letters were a room his body scared

He came to death with his mind drowning.
On the last day he enclosed himself
in a room with two bottles of gin, later
fell the length of his body
so that brain blood moved
to new compartments
that never knew the wash of fluid
and he died in minutes of a new equilibrium.

His early life was a terrifying comedy
and my mother divorced him again and again.
He would rush into tunnels magnetized
by the white eye of trains
and once, gaining instant fame,
managed to stop a Perahara in Ceylon
—the whole procession of elephants dancers
local dignitaries—by falling
dead drunk onto the street.

As a semi-official, and semi-white at that,
the act was seen as a crucial
turning point in the Home Rule Movement
and led to Ceylon's independence in 1948.

(My mother had done her share too—
her driving so bad
she was stoned by villagers
whenever her car was recognized)

For 14 years of marriage
each of them claimed he or she
was the injured party.
Once on the Colombo docks
saying goodbye to a recently married couple
my father, jealous
at my mother's articulate emotion,
dove into the waters of the harbour
and swam after the ship waving farewell.
My mother pretending no affiliation
mingled with the crowd back to the hotel.

Once again he made the papers
though this time my mother
with a note to the editor
corrected the report—saying he was drunk
rather than broken hearted at the parting of friends.
The married couple received both editions
of *The Ceylon Times* when their ship reached Aden.

And then in his last years
he was the silent drinker,
the man who once a week
disappeared into his room with bottles
and stayed there until he was drunk
and until he was sober.

There speeches, head dreams, apologies,
the gentle letters, were composed.
With the clarity of architects
he would write of the row of blue flowers
his new wife had planted,
the plans for electricity in the house,
how my half-sister fell near a snake
and it had awakened and not touched her.
Letters in a clear hand of the most complete empathy
his heart widening and widening and widening
to all manner of change in his children and friends
while he himself edged
into the terrible acute hatred
of his own privacy
till he balanced and fell
the length of his body
the blood screaming in
the empty reservoir of bones
the blood searching in his head without metaphor

bpNICHOL

---

b. 1944

1335 Comox Avenue

in fall
we lose ourselves
in new rooms, gaze
from windows grown old
in that season

we choose
new beds
to love in, cover our bodies
in confusions
of all
that should be left
behind

bury our faces in each other
tasting flesh in mouth
gathering warmth
possessing each other
as a way of loving

we are too near the sea
we hear the gulls cry
cars pass
the horns of ships
and cry
to see the moss grown

throw windows open
to night   to kneel   to pray
hands on each other
pressing body into body
some sort of liturgy

hear the sea   the bells
the sound of people passing
voices drifting up
and cold winds come
to chill our naked hearts

love is some sort of fire
come to warm us
fill our bodies
all in these motions
flowing into each other
in despair   the room
one narrow world
that might be anywhere

Dada Lama

TO THE MEMORY OF HUGO BALL

1

hweeeee
hweeeee
hyonnnn
hyonnnn

hweeeee
hweeeee
hyonnnn
hyonnnn

tubadididdo
tubadididdo
hyon
hyon

tubadididdo
tubadididdo
hyon
hyon

fffffffffffffffffffffffftsssssssss
ffffffffffffffffffffffffitssssssssss
ffffffffffffffffffffffffflitssssssssss

hyonnnnnn
          unh
hyonnnnnn
          unh

2

eeeeeeeeeeeeeeeeeeeeeeeeeeee
EEEEEEEEEEEEEEEEEEEEEEEEEEEE
eeeeeeeeeeeeeeeeeeeeeeeeeeee

EEEEEEEEEEEEEEEEEEEEEEEEEEEE
eeeeeeeeeeeeeeeeeeeeeeeeeeee
EEEEEEEEEEEEEEEEEEEEEEEEEEEE

eeeeeeeeeeeeeeeeeeeeeeeeeeee
EEEEEEEEEEEEEEEEEEEEEEEEEEEE
eeeeeeeeeeeeeeeeeeeeeeeeeeee

3

oudoo doan doanna
tinna limn limn
la leen
untloo lima
limna doo doo

dee du deena
deena dee du
deena deena
dee du deena

ah-ooo runtroo
lintle leave lipf
lat lina tanta
tlalum cheena
ran tron tra troo

deena dee du
deena deena
dee du deena
deena dee du

da dee di do du
deena
      deena

4

AAAAAAAAAAAAAAAAAAAAAA
a a a a a a a a a a a a a a a a a a a a a
AAAAAAAAAAAAAAAAAAAAAA

a a a a a a a a a a a a a a a a a a a a a
AAAAAAAAAAAAAAAAAAAAAA
a a a a a a a a a a a a a a a a a a a a a

AAAAAAAAAAAAAAAAAAAAAA
a a a a a a a a a a a a a a a a a a a a a
AAAAAAAAAAAAAAAAAAAAAA

5

tlic
tloc

tlic tloc
tlic tloc

tlic tloc tlic
tloc tlic tloc

tlic tloc tlic tloc
tlic tloc tlic tloc

tlic tloc tlic tloc tlic
tloc tlic tloc tlic tloc

tlic tloc tlic tloc tlic tloc
tlic tloc tlic tloc tlic tloc

tlic tloc tlic tloc tlic
tloc tlic tloc tlic tloc

tlic tloc tlic tloc
tlic tloc tlic tloc

tlic tloc tlic
tloc tlic tloc

tlic tloc
tlic tloc

tlic
tloc

6

wwwwwwwwwwwwwwwwwwwwwwwwwww
mmmmmmmmmmmmmmmmmmmmmmmmmmmmmmm
wwwwwwwwwwwwwwwwwwwwwwwwwwww
mmmmmmmmmmmmmmmmmmmmmmmmmmmmmmm

Wwwwwwwwwwwwwwwwwwwwwwwwww
Mmmmmmmmmmmmmmmmmmmmmmmmmmmmmmm
Wwwwwwwwwwwwwwwwwwwwwwwwwww
Mmmmmmmmmmmmmmmmmmmmmmmmmmmmmmm

WWWWWWWWWWWWWWWWWWWWWWWWWW
MMMMMMMMMMMMMMMMMMMMMMM
WWWWWWWWWWWWWWWWWWWWWWWWWWW

OUOOOOOOOOOOOOOOOOOOOOOOH
MMMMMMMMMMMMMMMMMMMMMMMMMMMM
OUOOOOOOOOOOOOOOOOOOOOOOOH
MMMMMMMMMMMMMMMMMMMMMMMMMMMM

FREEEEEEEEEEEEEEEEEEEEEEEEE
EEEAAAAAAAAAAAAAAAAAAAAAAAAAAAAAAH
FREEEEEEEEEEEEEEEEEEEEEEEEE
EEEAAAAAAAAAAAAAAAAAAAAAAAAAAAAAAH

FREEEEEEEEEEEEEEEEEEEEEEEEE
DUMMMMMMMMMMMMMMMMMMMMMMMMM
FREEEEEEEEEEEEEEEEEEEEEEEEE
DUMMMMMMMMMMMMMMMMMMMMMMMMM

Blues

```
                        l           e
                        o         e
              l   o   v   e
                o     e   v   o   l
        l   o   v   e         l
                e   v   o   l
          e   e       o
      e               l
```

late night summer poem

one of those nights the chest aches with emptiness
which part of me is missing?
                              what?

today i am writing these words

tomorrow i make them a poem

in lieu of a letter
i say what is least important
talk
        around the plain
truth

            it is fear
moves me to say these things

skirting the edge
i've skirted before
conscious always
i am not conscious of
the edge

                hello.

some strangers hands i make my own

with feeling
* *

if the body fills out
it fills out with love

if it is empty
it is full of the loving of emptiness

always there are spaces

always there are places we go to feeling certain things
lovingly finger familiar sorrows
& cling

* *

sorrow's a luxury
you fill up with poems

love you have little of
& use more sparingly

none of which is true

when you love others you love them with words & fingers
enter to give them those things you can
& when you have such nothing
you love only yourself
you fill your poems with self-love & loathing
& it is not poetry
       it is dead

* *

the poem begins & ends nowhere
being part of the flow you live with
starts when you're born
stepping in & out of
such moments you are aware
emerge as pages put in a book & titled
living always on the edges of
you are drawn into & cannot encompass
the flow of which is poetry

A Small Song That Is His

adore adore
adore adore
an opening an o
an h a leg a table or
a window & a w
a sky that is d
a lake that is f
e

d e f
f f f f
d d
   e e e
d f f e f e
f e f e

me
you or me or
i h & d
m e
e f d
o

d f h e w

f

f e w h d

o

w d

f

Two Words: A Wedding

FOR ROB & SHERON

There are things you have words for, things you do not have
words for. There are words that encompass all your feelings
& words that encompass none. There are feelings you have
that are like things to you, picked up & placed in the pocket,
worn like the cloth the pocket is attached to, like a skin you
live inside of. There is a body of feeling, of language, of
friends; the body politic, the body we are carried inside of till
birth, the body we carry our self inside of till death, a body
of knowledge that tells of an afterlife, a heaven, an unknown
everything we have many words for but cannot encompass.
There are relationships between words & concepts, between
things, between life & death, between friends & family,
between each other & some other other. We wed words to
things, people to feelings, speak of a true wedding of the
mind & heart, intuition & intellect, & out of this form our
realities. Our realities are wedded one to another, concepts
& people are joined, new people conceived within that mesh
of flesh & realities, are carried forward in the body of the
mother, the family, the bodily love we have for one another.
They are creating their own reality each step of the way,
daily, another kind of reality is born, each new word,
person, expanding our vocabulary, our concepts, new realities
are conceived, our old reality changes, the 'real' grows
realer every day. We are marrying the flesh to the flesh, the
word to the daily flux of lives we know & don't know, our
friends grow older & marry, raise children as you once were
children with mothers & fathers of your own, grow older, so
many things you still lack words for, struggle to wed the
inner & outer worlds, the self to some other self or selves,
confess your love & struggle with one another, together,
conscious there is this word is you, your name, & that you
are yet another thing or things you will never encompass,
never exhaust the possibilities of, because you are wedded to
the flux of life, because we are words and our meanings
change.

6:35 a.m. to 7:35 a.m.

                                            briefly

the heart does break

the aching muscle in the chest
carries more than the weight hangs from the body
                        from the barely perceiving brain
buried under the weight of loss

of grief

                    brief moment of clarity

                                        stillborn
i never know him
never name him
bury him under the greening tree in the shadow of the
    old stone wall

falls away from us

into the earth at birth

unborn again

                        when our son died
                        i feared ellie'd die too

                        a gnawing in the mind

                        blind terror

                        i held her all night
                        just to keep her to me

tho the heart pounds
the will shatters

you are broken

                                  his spirit dead

                                  our spirit

            in this world

oo quick

            without explanation

                                          gone

            drove into the countryside
            hours on the road to point pelée
            south to the very bottom
            skipped stones onto the lake
            flick across the surface &

                                          gone

to another world

ke my sister donna
ead at six weeks

                  or ellie's brother robert
                  dead at two years

to the slow dissolve of memory

life

            love's loss

                              passes

this grief

                        's past

in time

                    caring
                    awake all night &

past us

slipped thru that gap between the living & the dead

on

                    past this passing & this grief's hold

gone who was never ours to hold

                                        past us

briefly

                a life

                            time's alike

less thru loss

& yet

> the loss at last passes too

of us

> no "baby makes three"

> > not ours

alive or dead

> illusion of possession slips past us

GOD IT ALL SLIPS PAST US

so briefly

LOUIS DUDEK

1918-

Louis Dudek was born 6 February 1918 in Montreal. He completed a B.A. at McGill University and an M.A. and Ph.D. at Columbia University. He has taught modern poetry, Canadian literature, and European literature at McGill University for the past thirty years. A firm believer in the efficacy of the little magazine and the small press, Dudek has been involved in many non-commercial publishing enterprises. In the 1940s he worked with John Sutherland and Irving Layton in producing the little magazine *First Statement;* in the 1950s he joined with Raymond Souster and Layton in founding and running Contact Press while also participating in the editing of the magazine *CIV/n* (1953-54) and editing his own magazine *Delta* (1957-66). He worked with Glen Siebrasse and Michael Gnarowski in the 1960s, running Delta Canada Press, and ran DC Books with Aileen Collins in the 1970s.

Throughout his career Dudek's poetry has evinced a constant evolution. Of the poets of his generation, he has been the one who has strived the most for an epic scope in his work. His poetry represents an important contribution to the theory and practice of the Canadian avant-garde.

In his early work (*Unit of Five*, *East of the City*) Dudek concerned himself with writing a socially realistic poetry that emphasized a Marxist orientation. Having been brought up in a working class family, he saw social equality as an important stage in the evolution of Western civilization. In an early essay, "Academic Poetry" (1943), he argued against the Ivory Tower notion of poetry and called for poetry to be used as an important tool of political and social change.

Dudek's work of the early 1950s registered the influences of Ezra Pound (with whom he carried on an extensive correspondence) and Lionel Trilling (with whom he studied at Columbia University). In *Europe* he began to turn his attention away from human society and towards the world of art, the lasting artifacts that an imperfect and unperfectable society had produced.

In his pioneering long poems—*Europe, En Mexico,* and *Atlantis*—Dudek attempted to formulate epic assessments of human culture and evolution. His most recent work, *Continuation I*—an associative record of the individual mind at work—is a further contribution to the canon of non-narrative long poems that Dudek initiated. Although the long poem has been the main focus of his poetic attention over the past thirty years, he has also published a book of memorable satires *(Laughing Stalks)*, a book of epigrams *(Epigrams),* and two collections of evocative lyrics *(The Transparent Sea* and *Cross-Section).*

In spite of the ideational structures of his longer poems, Dudek has always favoured a direct mode of expression. Much of his poetry has attempted to wrestle back the power of statement that poetry has lost to prose in this century. Eschewing traditional forms, Dudek has utilized a sculpted shapeliness for his free verse poems. Several of his poems that take the sea for their subject ("Coming Suddenly to the Sea," "Europe 95," and the epilogue from *Atlantis)* have a hypnotic meditative quality and stand as some of the finest poems written in Canada in this century.

Dudek's works include *East of the City* (1946); *Europe* (1954; *The Transparent Sea* (1956); *En Mexico* (1958); *Laughing Stalks* (1958); *Literature and the Press* (1960); *Atlantis* (1967); *Collected Poetry* (1971); *Selected Essays and Criticism* (1978); *Cross-Section: Poems 1940-1980* (1980); and *Continuation I* (1981).

Works on Dudek include Wynne Francis, "A Critic of Life: Louis Dudek as a Man of Letters," *Canadian Literature,* No. 22 (1964), pp. 5-23; Dorothy Livesay, "The Sculpture of Poetry," *Canadian Literature,* No. 30 (1966), pp. 26-35; Douglas Barbour, "Poet as Philosopher," *Canadian Literature,* No. 53 (1972), pp. 18-29; Eva Seidner, "Modernism in the Booklength Poems of Louis Dudek," *Open Letter,* 3rd ser., No. 7 (1977), 14-40; and Frank Davey, *Louis Dudek & Raymond Souster* (1980).

— KEN NORRIS

AL PURDY

1918-

Alfred Wellington Purdy was born in Wooler, Ontario, and was educated in Trenton and Belleville. He served in the RCAF, and has held a number of blue-collar positions, chiefly in Vancouver and Montreal. Though settling at Roblin Lake, Ontario, in 1957, he has travelled extensively in Canada and abroad, an ongoing activity. He began writing poetry in adolescence; his first book was published in 1944 and he received the Governor-General's Award for *The Cariboo Horses* (1965). Purdy's further distinctions include Canada Council fellowships and writer-in-residencies, while his other work involves radio plays, reviews, essays, and several edited collections.

In the 1960s Purdy developed away from the conventional expression and sentiments of his early verse to his now-distinctive and accessible open-form poems. His mature poetry reveals the process of self-discovery; it is aural and oral, featuring an often talkative or anecdotal voice whose personality may be familiar, vital, and humorous. as well as formal, affected, or sombre in tone. Irony, often self-directed, is a major device, as is juxtaposition—of tones and times, of sorts and conditions. Purdy has an often confessional honesty in his resolutely colloquial language, though sudden metaphorical statements of great beauty and aphoristic insights may contrast with occasional, unapologetic rhetorical flourishes. He largely forgoes standard punctuation, as suits his refusal of codes and absolutes, and in keeping with the flow of associations in his poems. He also feels little compulsion to end any poem's process conclusively—though its ideas usually have an implied closure. Purdy wears his considerable learning lightly, and his poems appear deceptively simple and un-studied, as the forthright autobiographical reflections of a clear personality. However, his characteristic informality and sometimes wry, whimsical wit do not disguise his wisdom. Purdy's sometime meditative or speculative side is not arcane or pretentious, but is often set in seemingly informal recital and rooted in particular experience of the here-and-now. He always has a firm sense of what creates the identity of person or place, and of relationships across time. To Purdy the past serves as authentication and confirmation in the present of the fundamental continuity of humanity. His sympathies can become profound in recognizing human limits; he has a social and humane awareness that resists complete sentimental identity, for he is too consistently honest, even cautionary, for complete self-denial. Purdy's poetry is ultimately a vivacious but eloquent testimony to life and endurance, one that affirms the alternatives.

Purdy's works include *Poems for All the Annettes* (1962); *The Cariboo Horses* (1965); *North of Summer* (1967); *Wild Grape Wine* (1968); *Sex and Death* (1973); *In Search of Owen Roblin* (1974); *Sundance at Dusk* (1976); *No Other Country* (1977); *Being Alive: Poems 1958-1978* (1978); and *The Stone Bird* (1981).

Works on Purdy include George Bowering, *Al Purdy* (1970); Peter Stevens, "In the Raw: The Poetry of A. W. Purdy," *Canadian Literature*, No. 28 (1966), pp. 22-30; George Woodcock, "On the Poetry of Al Purdy," in *Al Purdy, Selected Poems* (1972); Mike Doyle, "Proteus at Roblin Lake," *Canadian Literature*, No. 61 (1974), pp. 7-23; and Ants Riego, "The Purdy Poem," *Canadian Literature*, No. 79 (1978), pp. 127-31.

– LOUIS K. MACKENDRICK

RAYMOND SOUSTER

1921-

Raymond Souster was born in Toronto's west end and, except

for four years in the RCAF during World War II, has spent most of his life in that neighbourhood. After graduating from high school in 1939, he was employed by the Imperial Bank which merged eventually with the Commerce. He is now custodian of the Securities Department. After a few years of apprenticeship during which he printed poems on a mimeograph machine in the basement of his house, Souster became associated with the renaissance of poetry in Montreal during the late 1940s and the 1950s. Along with Louis Dudek and Irving Layton he founded and edited the influential Contact Press. That triumvirate was instrumental in bringing into Canadian poetry the ideas of craft and subject espoused by American poets. As an editor, Souster has worked on several literary magazines including *Direction* (1943-46) and *Combustion* (1957-60), as well as on anthologies of emerging poets such as *Poets 56* (1956), *New Wave Canada* (1966), and *Made in Canada* (1970). An early edition of collected poems, *The Colour of the Times*, won the 1964 Governor-General's Award for poetry, and his 1979 collection, *Hanging In*, won the City of Toronto Book Award. Souster was instrumental in the formation of the League of Canadian Poets in 1966, and twice has served as its chairman. Souster is best known as "the Toronto poet" because much of his work is concerned with recording life in that city. In focussing on one place and exploring it, he is following an idea of William Carlos Williams' *(Paterson)* that this should be one of a poet's duties and goals. For Souster, Toronto is a microcosm of the world. It has quiet beauty (the west end, the Islands, treelined sidestreets, first snowfalls on flower beds, birds in blossoming Japanese cherry trees) and horrific ugliness (the financial towers, hollow lives, pasty faces, neon, grit, rooming houses, parkettes strewn with empty wine bottles). These and other aspects of the city may be found in separate poems, but they are two sides of the same coin. Souster's vision of the world turns on their co-existence and the relationship between them. Thus, his vision is essentially an ironic one in which the best of life and the worst of life battle constantly for attention. It is important to know that, although this viewpoint has been nourished in and by Toronto, it was first made clear to Souster during World War II when he experienced the paradox of cameraderie and attrition. His war poems complement his Toronto poems to produce an appreciation of joy or even of quiet satisfaction against a backdrop of ugliness and death. Souster does not fear the overtly sentimental or nostalgic; indeed much of his work involves an interplay between innocence and experience—especially in regard to his own childhood. In developing a voice to express this world-view, he has transformed the influence of Ezra Pound, Williams, Charles Olson, and Wallace Stevens into poems that are marked by at once a sureness and diversity of tone, rhythm, and form— from the imagistic to the purely conversational. Although some critics find it difficult to grant Souster the status of an important poet—accusing him of diffuseness and unalloyed didacticism—there are many others who recognize the diversity, relevance, and vitality of both his subjects and his expression. Perhaps finally he is a poet who feels acutely and can communicate effectively the small moments in life that most people do not notice, but eventually come to recognize as important, to appreciate, or to fear.

Souster's works include *Unit of Five* (1944); *When We Are Young* (1946); *Shake Hands with the Hangman* (1953); *For What Time Slays* (1955); *A Local Pride* (1962); *The Colour of the Times* (1964); *Selected Poems* (1972); *Extra Innings* (1977); *Hanging In* (1979); and *The Collected Poems of Raymond Souster* (Volume 1, 1980; Volume 2, 1981).

Works on Souster include Louis Dudek, "Groundhog among the Stars: The Poetry of Raymond Souster," *Canadian Literature*, No. 22 (1964), pp. 34-49; Gary Geddes, "A Cursed and Singular Blessing," *Canadian Literature*, No. 54 (1972), pp. 27-36; Hugh Cook, "Development in the Early Poetry of Raymond Souster," *Studies in Canadian Literature*, 3 (1978), 113-18; and Francis Mansbridge, "A Delicate Balance: Craft in Raymond Souster's Poetry," *Canadian Poetry: Studies, Documents, Reviews*, No. 4 (1979), pp. 45-51.

– ROBERT BILLINGS

ELI MANDEL

1922-

Estevan, Saskatchewan, Eli Mandel's birthplace, is the subject
and title of one of his most-anthologized poems and source-place
for the poems in *Out of Place*. Moving to Regina in 1932, he
returned there after World War II medical corps service to take a
B.A. and M.A. at the University of Saskatchewan. Following
four year's teaching at Collège Militaire Royale de St. Jean,
Quebec, during which time his first book, *Trio*, appeared,
he completed his Ph.D. (University of Toronto, 1957), and
joined the University of Alberta (Edmonton) English Department. He remained there for nine years with the exception of
one year (1963-64) at York University, Toronto, where he is now
Professor of English and Humanities. In 1967, *An Idiot Joy* won
the Governor-General's Award for Poetry. The publication of
Stony Plain followed a sabbatical in Europe, and *Life Sentence:
Poems and Journals 1976-1980* draws in part on travels in Peru,
India, and Europe. An influential critic and anthologer as well
as poet, Mandel was made a Fellow of the Royal Society of
Canada in 1982.

The title of Eli Mandel's most recent book, *Life Sentence*,
might be taken as descriptive of his concerns throughout his
career. The prisons within prisons the poet and all of us are
trapped in — families, cultures, politics, religions, metaphysical and philosophic systems — are labyrinths and cages constructed by language, the same language the poet is sentenced
to use as a means of freeing himself. The physical body is
tortured by speech. Condemnation and self-condemnation,
betrayal and self-betrayal, are thus recurrent themes, as riddle and paradox are recurrent poetic techniques. Humankind
creates apparently rational orders and pretends to a civility
which denies yet is denied by the monstrous perversity of
human nature itself. Goya's "The dream of reason brings

forth monsters" could well stand as a motto for Mandel's work; certainly minotaurs, bird-men and -women, and other versions of human-animal creatures inhabit his poems, images of divided self, labyrinthine language. Structures of words and structures of power are apparatuses of romance and melodrama we design to deny death, perpetuate illusions; pollutants which keep us from seeing each other's gestures, receiving each other's messages. If the poet is marked by his place of origin, that place is equally the shifting plain of language. Mandel's response to place (seen at its simplest in his found poems) is usually to imagine someone or something *out* of place, an acute sense, related at times to his Judaism, of being alien. Mandel's poetic structures are palinodial and parodic: structures of denial and doubleness. His frequent use of reflexive images — things within things, reflecting worlds and mirrors — is symbolic of the mind's ability both to imagine complex systems and to box itself in. His use of personae and his sometimes difficult syntax indicate his refusal to accept simple summaries, final solutions. But Mandel has an often overlooked gift for writing graceful lyrics, in which clarity, openness, and freedom are possibilities sung of in songs, songs to which we can't quite remember the words.

Mandel's works include *Fuseli Poems* (1960); *Black and Secret Man* (1964); *An Idiot Joy* (1967); *Stony Plain* (1973); *Crusoe* (1973); *Out of Place* (1977); *Dreaming Backwards* (1981); *Life Sentence* (1981); and the critical books *Irving Layton* (1969, 1981), *Another Time* (1977).

Works on Mandel include Michael Higgins, "Eli Mandel, Poet of the Prairies," *The Chelsea Journal*, 4, No. 1 (1978), 38-44; Kenneth Sherman, "Inside Out," *Waves*, 10, No. 4 (1982), 77-80; David Staines, "Eli Mandel's Investigations," *Book Forum*, 4, No. 1 (1978), 139-43; Peter Stevens, "Poet as Critic as Prairie Poet, "*Essays on Canadian Writing*, Nos. 18-19 (1980), pp. 54-69; and Andrew Suknaski, "Out of *narayan* to *bifrost*/ the word,"*Brick*, No. 14 (1981), pp. 5ff.

— ANN MANDEL

MILTON ACORN

1923-

Milton Acorn was born in Charlottetown, Prince Edward Island. Trained as a carpenter, he gave up carpentry in 1956 to become a full-time poet. In Montreal he met Irving Layton and Al Purdy who were important influences on him. In 1963, after a period in Toronto and the failure of his marriage to Gwendolyn MacEwen, he moved to Vancouver where he was active in the West Coast political and literary scene. He returned to Toronto in the late sixties and in 1970 a number of fellow poets created the "Canadian Poetry Award" for him and named him "The People's Poet" in recognition of *I've Tasted My Blood* (1969). Acorn won the Governor-General's Award for *The Island Means Minago* (1975). He now lives in Charlottetown.

Acorn is one of Canada's few committed Marxist poets and certainly its best. His poetry displays a wide range of interests apparently unrelated to politics—nature, love, friendship, and poetry itself are particularly important themes—but underlying his work is a central concern which is essentially political. Acorn sees life as a process of definition through struggle, and his deepest commitment is to the dialectical process as it expresses itself through all aspects of existence from the broadest political movements to the most minute details of the natural world. Acorn's dialectical vision determines his concept of the poet's role which finds its most profound and moving expression in his elegy for Red Lane, "Words Said Sitting on a Rock Sitting on a Saint." Acorn has one of the finest lyric gifts of any Canadian poet. His best poems are especially outstanding for their rhythmic subtlety deriving ultimately from the patterns of the spoken word. Acorn's imagery is also remarkable, both for its precision and its evocativeness. At moments of greatest intensity, generally moments when the dialectical process of conflict and resolution is at its height, image and rhythm seem to combine and expand organically into verse paragraphs extending over many lines. Acorn is often far from his best, especially in much of the political poetry of the late sixties and seventies. His sense of himself as a public persona is very evident in this period and the poems, with some exceptions, suffer from a general coarsening of thought, structure, and texture. There is an abstract rootless quality to much of this work which is in stark contrast to Acorn's earlier lyrics, in which he showed himself a master at expressing his political vision through the nuances of particular personal experiences. However, many of the poems in his latest volume, *Jackpine Sonnets*, show a renewal of the control and power which had been largely missing from his work for years.

Acorn's works include *In Love and Anger* (1956); *The Brain's the Target* (1960); *Against a League of Liars* (a broadsheet) (1961); a special issue of *The Fiddlehead* containing fifty-eight poems (1963); *Jawbreakers* (1963); *I've Tasted My Blood: Poems 1956 to 1968* (1969); *I Shout Love and On Shaving Off His Beard* (1971); *More Poems for People* (1972); *The Island Means Minago* (1975); and *Jackpine Sonnets* (1977).

Works on Acorn include M. Gnarowski, "Milton Acorn: A Review in Retrospect," *Culture*, 25 (1964), 119-29; and Dorothy Livesay, "Search for a Style: The Poetry of Milton Acorn," *Canadian Literature*, No. 40 (1969), pp. 33-42.

– ZAILIG POLLOCK

JAMES REANEY

1926-

James Reaney grew up on a farm near Stratford, Ontario, to which he regularly returns. He received his B.A. (1948), M.A. (1949), and Ph.D. (1958) from the University of To-

288

ronto. He has taught English at the University of Manitoba (1949-56; 1958-60) and at the University of Western Ontario (1960 to the present). He won the Governor-General's Award for his first volume, *The Red Heart* (1949) and has won it three times since. He has edited his own magazine, *Alphabet* (1960-71), directed an experimental theatre centre, written for both the adult and children's theatre, collaborated with composer John Beckwith and artist Jack Chambers, and written many critical articles. His wife, Colleen Thibaudeau, is also a poet.

The conclusion of "The School Globe" catalogues the contrasting images in *The Red Heart*, just as "The Red Heart" and "Antichrist as a Child" embody the two modes of perception of the central poet-figure of that volume. But all these opposites are not irreconcilable, and the impetus of Reaney's development has been toward a reconciliation. The destructive energy of "The Sun Dogs" already suggests a divine vision in the burning trees. Though "a ring / Around the moon" traditionally prefigures disaster, the children see it as a game, and, like the children, the poet sees the inversion of social forms as a creative outburst of masculine energy, confirmed by the reappearance of this poem in *Colours in the Dark* in close association with the father. Feminine luxuriance lulls the child in "The Plum Tree," in "the room where he was born."

Still, Reaney tells us that he lacked the ability to organize these opposites within an enclosing "design" until he studied Spenser, Blake, Yeats, and the criticism of Northrop Frye. The design is that of language and literatures themselves as depicted in "The Alphabet," which rises from letters signifying sounds to levels of metaphoric complexity ending with letters enclosing, in a type of emblem, all the Bible from Adam and Eve to the new Jerusalem. Similarly inclusive structures organize the familiar details of the Ontario landscape in "April Eclogue" and "To the Avon River." Reaney concludes *Twelve Letters* with a circular motif and a Virgilian echo: "In short, everything was / The bicycle of which I sing." "The Wheel" is another metaphor of epic, encyclopaedic inclusiveness. "The red buggy wheels move so fast /

They stand still," in a fusion of all the opposites in the poem. *The Gyroscope* (1981), a play that explores the nature of poetry, has a similar motif as its title. Germaine Warkentin rightly finds the encyclopaedia the dominant structural motif of the later Reaney; it is implicit in the earliest work as well.

Reaney's work includes *The Red Heart* (1949); *A Suit of Nettles* (1958); *The Killdeer and Other Plays* (1962); *Twelve Letters to a Small Town* (1962); *The Dance of Death at London, Ontario* (1963); *Colours in the Dark* (1969); *Listen to the Wind* (1972); *Poems* (1972); *Applebutter and Other Plays for Children* (1973); and *The Donnellys* (1975-77).

Works on Reaney include Alvin A. Lee, *James Reaney* (1969); Ross G. Woodman, *James Reaney* (1972); Margaret Atwood, "Reaney Collected," *Canadian Literature*, No. 57 (1973), pp. 113-17; Germaine Warkentin, Introductions to *Poems* (1972), *Selected Shorter Poems* (1975), and *Selected Longer Poems* (1976); and Stan Dragland, ed., *Approaches to the Work of James Reaney* (1982).

— RICHARD STINGLE

ROBERT KROETSCH

1927-

Robert Kroetsch was born and spent his early years in Heisler, Alberta. As the son of a struggling prairie farmer he came to know intimately the geography and people who appear so frequently in his poetry and fiction. After receiving his B.A. from the University of Alberta in 1948 he worked on riverboats in the Northwest Territories until 1951, when he became a civilian education and information specialist for the U.S. Army. From 1954-55 he did graduate work at McGill University and then received his M.A. from Middlebury College in 1956. After obtaining his Ph.D. from the University of Iowa in 1961, he joined the Department of English at the State University of New York at Binghampton. In 1978 he returned to Canada to teach at the University of Manitoba.

The predominantly short lyrics in *The Stone Hammer Poems 1960-1975* demonstrate Kroetsch's persistent attempt to understand the spatial, temporal, and linguistic impulses shaping his double career as writer and teacher. Kroetsch's attraction to doubled experience emerges in his early use of a three-line stanza with split, binary lines. *The Stone Hammer Poems* also show Kroetsch's concern with developing a prairie-oriented sense of "local pride" which would articulate a "dream of origins" and "tell *our* story" by speaking in "the grammar of our days." This "grammar," which is Post-Modern and processive, embodies the dialectical tensions central to Kroetsch's work: past and present fuse, love announces loss, voice and vision blend, death embraces life. Ultimately the dialectic is between creation and creator ("art, man, art") as much as it is about "the uncertain / principles of time and space."

With the publication of *The Ledger* (1975), and later in *Seed Catalogue* (1977) and *The Sad Phoenician* (1979), Kroetsch assumed fully the role of oral poet and shaman "in a world that didn't have shamans": increasingly he tested the possibilities offered by the long poem which, "by its very length, allows the exploration of the failure of system and grid." In exploring this failure Kroetsch finds room for serious narrative play: he pursues contradiction; he juggles metaphor and "fact"; he invents through parataxis; he breaks, renews, destroys. Here the open-ended process celebrates the prairie poet's ability to put "space all over the place." Equally, it asserts Kroetsch's resistance to closure; it confirms his attraction to language as an erotic, intoxicating force; it allows him to throw the poem's focus out to echoing planes of reference; and it lets him revel in the options offered by the storytelling act. At once colloquial, anecdotal, and formally complex, Kroetsch's most involved verse articulates a radical theory of writing in which the poet finds both "a dispatch of silence" as well as "the destruction that allows the new."

Kroetsch's works include *But We Are Exiles* (1965); *The Words of my Roaring* (1966); *The Studhorse Man* (1969);

Gone Indian (1973); *Badlands* (1975); *The Stone Hammer Poems 1960-1975* (1975); *The Ledger* (1975); *Seed Catalogue* (1977); *What the Crow Said* (1978); and *Field Notes* (1981).

Works on Kroetsch include Russell M. Brown, "An Interview with Robert Kroetsch," *University of Windsor Review*, 7, No. 2 (Spring 1972), 1-18; Morton L. Ross, "Robert Kroetsch and His Novels," in *Writers of the Prairies*, ed. Donald G. Stephens (1973); Robert Enright and Dennis Cooley, "Uncovering Our Dream World: An Interview with Robert Kroetsch," *Arts Manitoba*, 1, No. 1 (Jan.-Feb. 1977), 32-39; Robert Lecker, "Robert Kroetsch's Poetry," *Open Letter*, 3rd Ser., No. 8 (Spring 1978), 72-88; and Peter Thomas, *Robert Kroetsch* (1980).

– ROBERT LECKER

PHYLLIS WEBB

1927-

Phyllis Webb was born in Victoria, British Columbia, and spent her early years there and in Vancouver where she studied at the University of British Columbia. Her political interests surfaced when she ran as a CCF candidate in provincial elections. When she moved to Montreal in the 1950s, her political and literary concerns flourished, resulting in her first book publication. She then lived for some years in Europe, eventually returning to Vancouver. She became the producer of the CBC's Ideas Network based in Toronto. After her resignation from that program, she went to live on the Gulf Islands in British Columbia.

Phyllis Webb's poetry presents a remote world refined to a bleakness, and yet such bleakness is tempered by a complex irony. The poet accepts the dark side of existence yet concentrates on shaping her own responses within clearly defined limits. Such a search for the acceptance of despair as an ambience of existence not only urges the poems into contemplation of large universal movements and cycles expressed in images of sea and bones—often teased out in wittily intellectual terms—but also creates a poetry reduced to enclosed spaces with images of rooms and gardens. These clear boundaries are mirrored in her sharpening of form in order to discover the essence of existence. Her poetry, then, builds a swaying tension between an outer life of philosophical questioning concerned with historical and biological necessities, and her analysis of her relationships with others to define the meaning of any individual life. The use of deliberate structuring and stanzaic form serves as an attempt to control the irreconcilable demands imposed by both private and public life until the poems move to shorter, sheared-down forms, these concentrated pieces being for the poet a statement as temporary anchor in the tidal immensities of life. Sometimes the poet is able to express a positive note in starkly simple, almost imagistic terms, though often such expressions are deflected by their opposites. Such a dialectical and refining process reaches its minimal expression in the series, Naked Poems. While her bleak view of the world continues with her sense of personal, political, and social confinement in her uncompleted Kropotkin Poems (some of these poems, however, appear in her last volume, Wilson's Bowl), among her more recent poems are some which move into that personally evoked balance that is neatly summarized by the title of one such poem — "Eschatology of Spring." The language in her early poems was full of metaphor and figures, gradually shearing away, as she begins to distrust the traps language and syntax can set, towards a clarity of direct speech that occasionally breaks out into a colloquial, throw-away style.

Phyllis Webb's works include Trio: First Poems by Gael Turnbull, Phyllis Webb, E. W. Mandel (1954); Even Your Right Eye (1956); The Sea Is Also a Garden (1962); Naked Poems (1965); Selected Poems 1954-1965 (1971); and Wilson's Bowl (1980).

Works on Webb include Helen Sonthoff, "Structures of Loss: The Poetry of Phyllis Webb," Canadian Literature, No. 9 (1961), pp. 15-22; John Hulcoop, "Introduction," in Selected Poems

1954-1965 (1971); Frank Davey, "Phyllis Webb," *From There to Here* (1974); and Phyllis Webb, "Polishing Up the View," *CV/II*, 2 (1976), 14-15.

– PETER STEVENS

D. G. JONES

1929-

Born in Bancroft, Ontario in 1929, Douglas Gordon Jones teaches English at the Université de Sherbrooke. Educated at both McGill and Queen's Universities, he gained early recognition as a poet at McGill where his work was supported and published by Louis Dudek and Raymond Souster. As testimony to his achievement both as poet and critic, Jones was awarded the Governor-General's Award for *Under the Thunder the Flowers Light Up the Earth*, and the President's Medal (University of Western Ontario) for "The Lampman Poems." He is also a Fellow of the Royal Society of Canada, as well as a founding editor of *Ellipse*, a review devoted to publishing anglophone and francophone poetry in translation. He resides in North/Hatley, Quebec.

The cosmic focus of Jones' poetry, the centre around which it turns, is the figure of the sun and the enduring luminosity of the world. But it is a sun that at once destroys and creates, Lucifer, of whom it is asked in "Phrases from Orpheus": "Are / You / Light / or Dark?" From this ambiguous centre Jones proceeds with elegant care, his initial books addressing the sun as overlaid with frost and the sun as axeman. The life, then, that lies in nature's core is checked by a maleficent gesture. To reckon with such a cosmic order is the poet's task, and to aid himself in his enterprise he frequently invokes the history of art, both contemporary Canadian and European, as well as ancient Chinese. For it is painting that speaks directly of nature as an interplay of light and dark, and transposed to categories of thought they become forces of moral and psychological violence that form the predominant structures of Jones's poetry. Because of the difficulty of distinguishing light from dark at the source, the problem for the poet is to dramatize opposition, project an ambiguity, and so to manipulate irony that judgements remain suspended. As a result, Jones has forged an unmistakable tone and syntax that finely relates and distinguishes, a style whose desire "creates / a dream of limits / And it grows in gravity as that takes shape." Under the steady pressure to allow for the minutest shifts of perception, whose consequences are always of an unforeseeable magnitude, the apparently intellectual surface of the earlier poems yields to the play of language that has gradually made of the mind only one of the modes of perceiving the world. Thus his more recent poems are characterized by increased refinement and humorous juxtapositions ("7/4/75"). But delicately suspended between light and dark, one preoccupation remains constant through all of Jones's *oeuvre*: the immediacy of the land, a given that determines perspective and meaning. It is a landscape of language: "You are a figure on my horizon. We walk / together the horizons / of an old discourse." It is also a landscape, despite erosion and inevitable decay, where the world's renewal is the one celebration: "what's tough / . . . is raising from a holocaust / the rose with a green leaf." This is the poetry of mature pastoral whose praise springs always from catastrophe.

Jones's work includes *Frost on the Sun* (1957); *The Sun is Axeman* (1961); *Phrases From Orpheus* (1967); *Butterfly on Rock: A Study of Themes and Images in Canadian Literature* (1970); Paul-Marie Lapointe, *The Terror of the Snows: Selected Poems*, trans. D. G. Jones (1976); and *Under the Thunder the Flowers Light Up the Earth* (1977).

Works on Jones include E. D. Blodgett, "The Masks of D. G. Jones," *Canadian Literature*, No. 60 (1974); and George Bowering, "Coming Home to the World," *Canadian Literature*, No. 65 (1975).

— E. D. BLODGETT

JAY MACPHERSON

1931-

Born in England, Jay Macpherson came to Canada at the age of nine. After four years in St. John's, Newfoundland, she moved to Ottawa where she attended Glebe Collegiate and Carleton College from which she received her B.A. in 1951. In 1955 Macpherson received her M.A. from Victoria College, University of Toronto, with a thesis on "Milton and the Pastoral Tradition," and in 1964 her Ph.D. from the same University with a dissertation on "Narcissus, or the Pastoral of Solitude; Some Conventions of Nineteenth-Century Romance." She is now Associate Professor of English at Victoria College. Her first major collection of poems, *The Boatman* (1957), received a Governor-General's Award.

Jay Macpherson has been concerned from the beginning of her career with technical experimentation in traditional verse forms and with the construction of a personal thematics with its roots in biblical, Classical, and Sumerian mythologies, and the literature of the Romantic period. The great themes of the Fall, exile from the Promised Land, salvation and redemption, meet in a concern with Noah and Jonah, Adam and Eve, Tammuz and Narcissus, as well as the haunted selves of the Gothic novel and modern horror film. As D. G. Jones has observed in *Butterfly on Rock*, central to Macpherson's work is the recognition and acceptance of the "essentially sacrificial character of life," a preface necessary to the eventual affirmation of the world evident in the selections reprinted here from *The Boatman*. Before we can live in the world presented in the title poem of that volume, we must learn to contain our "beasts" rather than wrestle with them, and to follow the course of imaginative redemption traced in "The Fisherman" and "The Anagogic Man."

In *Welcoming Disaster*, however, that process is cast into doubt. Falada, the talking horse from Grimm's tale "The

Goose-Girl," here speaks not the truth as in the original but false and misleading words expressive of the path of deception which rules the world. Only by seeing through false prophecy and enduring disaster, understanding the true nature of "Hecate Trivia" and "Playing" by confronting our own ghosts and ghouls, can the treacherous cycle of betrayal and self-amputation be broken. One of the most starkly powerful poems in contemporary Canadian literature, *Welcoming Disaster* leaves us in little doubt that exile is the inevitable result of the vision of love in a fallen world.

Jay Macpherson's works include *Nineteen Poems* (1952); *O Earth Return* (1954); and *The Boatman* (1957; 1968). *The Boatman* was reprinted with *Welcoming Disaster* (1974) as *Poems Twice Told* (1982).

Works on Macpherson include James Reaney, "The Third Eye—Jay Macpherson's *The Boatman*," *Canadian Literature*, No. 3 (1960), pp. 23-34; D. G. Jones, *Butterfly on Rock* (1970); Northrop Frye, *The Bush Garden* (1971), pp. 70-75; and Suniti Namjoshi, "In the Whale's Belly—Jay Macpherson's Poetry," *Canadian Literature*, No. 79 (1978), pp. 54-59.

– LORRAINE WEIR

ALDEN NOWLAN

1933-

Alden Nowlan was born near Windsor, Nova Scotia, to an Irish rural working class background. He quit school in grade 5 and began to write stories and verses. Throughout his youth he did various labouring jobs. From 1952 to 1967 he worked as a newspaper reporter and editor, first in Hartland, New Brunswick, and later in Saint John. Nowlan published his first book of poems in 1958 and received a Canada Council Fellowship in 1961. In 1966 he underwent three operations for cancer of the throat. In 1967 Nowlan won the Governor-

General's Award for Poetry and received a Guggenheim Fellowship that enabled him, his wife Claudine, and their son Johnnie to travel to Ireland and England. Since 1968 Nowlan has been Writer-in-Residence at the University of New Brunswick.

Alden Nowlan was first regarded by readers of poetry as a regional realist—a man obsessed by the physical and psychological violence inherent in the puritanical way of life in the Maritime provinces. His style was thought to be flatly descriptive, austere, and fairly old-fashioned. In *Bread, Wine and Salt*, however, the critics found a new Alden Nowlan—a man who was now more concerned with tenderness than with violence, a poet whose style was now more effortless than formal, whose outlook was more humanistic than regional. The truth is, Nowlan has written from a consistent viewpoint and with a consistent vision from the beginning of his career. His viewpoint is that of a Maritimer: a person who respects the traditions of both history and folklore, who has experienced economic deprivation and the violent defeats and joyous triumphs poverty can engender, who takes a friendly and personal interest in the human condition, and who loves being home to celebrate or mourn with rum or religion, music or love. Nowlan's view of life concerns the problem of identity: the sense of being a stranger in one's own world, of feeling the sudden miraculous power or sudden humiliating impotence upon finding oneself in an unusual situation. Nowlan's best poems always present an image of reality being disturbed in such a way that a new identity offers itself to somebody. Usually the person fails to achieve, or even accept, the metamorphosis, and the result is a deep sense of pathos for the person and for the reader. Sometimes the person in the poem desires the impossible and the failure seems even sadder. Occasionally the person actually experiences a new identity and the effect on the reader is strange and wonderful. Far from being a realist, Nowlan has always written with a sacramental vision, an understanding of the heart's need for symbolic gestures and words to transform existence into meaning. Nowlan's simple diction, conversational rhythms, and friendly tone may be misleading. Though his style has become increasingly casual, his vision has never lapsed from the strongly imagined experience to the merely perceived one. Alden Nowlan has always believed that "to be a poet is to express what humans feel."

Nowlan's works include *Bread, Wine and Salt* (1967); *The Mysterious Naked Man* (1969); *Playing the Jesus Game* (1970); *Between Tears and Laughter* (1971); *I'm a Stranger Here Myself* (1974); *Smoked Glass* (1977); and *I Might Not Tell Everybody This* (1982). Related to his poetry is his fictional memoir, *Various Persons Named Kevin O'Brien* (1973), and his essay collection *Double Exposure* (1978).

Works on Nowlan include Louis Dudek, "A Reading of Two Poems by Alden Nowlan," *The Fiddlehead*, No. 81 (1969), pp. 51-59; Robert Bly, "For Alden Nowlan, with Admiration," *The Tamarack Review*, No. 54 (1970), pp 32-38; Peter Pacey, rev. of *Between Tears and Laughter*, *The Fiddlehead*, No. 93 (1972), pp. 114-16; Marilyn Baxter, "Wholly Drunk or Wholly Sober?", *Canadian Literature*, Nos. 68-69 (1976), pp. 106-11; and Michael Brian Oliver, *Poet's Progress: The Development of Alden Nowlan's Poetry* (1978).

– MICHAEL BRIAN OLIVER

JOE ROSENBLATT

1933-

Joe Rosenblatt was born in Toronto. He left school after Grade 10 and lived in British Columbia for seven years before returning to Toronto where he worked at various jobs and began to forge a literary career. As one of the poets to emerge out of the renaissance of Canadian literature in the late 1960s, he gained wide public notice as one of a group of poets led by Milton Acorn who campaigned to make Toronto's Allan Gardens a platform for free speech. *Top Soil*, a compilation of

Rosenblatt's early books, won the Governor-General's Award for poetry in 1976. The drawings with which he illustrates his books have been hung in several art galleries. He has been the editor of *Jewish Dialogue* since 1970. Rosenblatt has recently taken up permanent residence on Vancouver Island where he does some teaching in the Creative Writing Department at the University of Victoria, and is the poetry editor of *The Malahat Review*.

The early influences on Rosenblatt's work emerged out of the general loosening of form and structure initiated by William Carlos Williams, Ezra Pound, Charles Olson, and the Black Mountain school of poetry in the United States. Some of the tenets of this kind of poetry that can be seen in his work include paying attention to the actual *sounds* created by language, and the use of very liquid or freely moving language and patterns of thought. These and other elements combine with Rosenblatt's fascination with insects and animals to produce poems in which bees buzz across a page and imaginative transformations occur frequently and unpredictably. He believes the world of creatures can be used not only as a foil to the human world, but also as instructive in man's need to keep in touch with the cycles of life, especially regeneration. Further, Rosenblatt's bestiary can include mankind. The juxtapositions created by his vivid and exotic imagination have been compared to the "metaphysical" conceits of British poets of the Renaissance, specifically John Donne. Rosenblatt's drawings complement the vision presented in his poems: they are crowded with vegetation, creatures of various sizes and deformities, and symbols of regeneration. Under his often witty presentation of the instinctual, the bestial, and the absurd lies a deep concern for the lot of mankind. Rosenblatt wants us to overcome the great or small tragedies inherent in trying to cope with a violent, sometimes ridiculous world in order that we may retain the ability to perceive the wonder and intricacies of all forms of life.

Rosenblatt's works include *The LSD Leacock* (1966); *Winter of the Lunar Moth* (1968); *Bumblebee Dithyramb* (1972); *Dream Craters* (1974); *Virgins and Vampires* (1975); *Top Soil* (1976); *Tommy Fry and the Ant Colony* (1979); *The*

Sleeping Lady (1980); and *The Brides of the Stream* (1983).

Works on Rosenblatt include Fred Cogswell, "One Touch of Nature," *Canadian Literature*, No. 40 (1969), pp. 71-72; Frank Davey,"Joe Rosenblatt,"in *From There to Here*(1974) and Ed Jewinski, "Joe Rosenblatt," in *Canadian Writers and Their Works* (forthcoming, 1983).

— ROBERT BILLINGS

LEONARD COHEN

1934-

Leonard Cohen was born in Montreal and educated at McGill University. He dropped out of graduate school at Columbia University to write and to perform music in Montreal nightclubs. Now internationally known as a songwriter and entertainer, Cohen continues sporadically to publish books of poetry and prose. His *Selected Poems, 1956-1968* won the Governor-General's Award; Cohen declined the award. In recent years he has given few performances and recitations of his work. He continues to live in Montreal for part of the year, making frequent trips to the Continent.

Of all the Canadian poets of the Post-Modern period, Cohen appears to be the most confirmed formalist. All of his work draws the reader into a world of artifice in which style is the ultimate statement. Much of Cohen's work displays a thematic preoccupation with love, sex, and religion. His visionary novel, *Beautiful Losers*, conjured up images of transfiguration and transcendence, and his poetry reflects similar concerns. His first book, *Let Us Compare Mythologies*, introduced the reader to the rites of sexuality and worship in an atmosphere of semi-decadent pre-Raphaelitism.

In *The Spice Box of Earth* Cohen established himself as a believable modern Romantic. Primarily a book of love poems, *The Spice Box of Earth* is exquisitely lyrical and contains some of the most elegant love poems ("For Anne," "As the Mist Leaves No Scar," "Now of Sleeping") written in recent times.

The atmosphere of tenderness found in *The Spice Box of Earth* was quickly superseded, however, by the nightmarish world depicted in *Flowers for Hitler*. In this collection the world, for Cohen, has taken on the dimensions of a concentration camp. A transcendent religious atmosphere is replaced by one of worldly power; the reciprocal nature of love has now been transformed into a struggle between master and slave.

In *Flowers for Hitler* Cohen replaced ritualized lushness with surrealistic effects. In *The Energy of Slaves* he stripped his poetry entirely of what he has called "my own Baroque." The poems are stark and pointed, continuing to present a world dominated by power relationships and spiritual devastation.

Cohen's most recent book, *Death of a Lady's Man*, seems to be a first attempt at reconciling the romantic and holocaust visions that Cohen has alternately embraced. The book exists as a concert of voices, with most of the poems and prose being followed by a "commentary" which highlights, contradicts, or criticizes the original piece. The effect is one of being presented with a variety of perspectives and systems of thought with which to view art and life. The multi-faceted quality of the book would appear to signal a growing harmony and integration in Cohen's poetic world.

Cohen's works include *Let Us Compare Mythologies* (1956); *The Spice Box of Earth* (1961); *The Favorite Game* (1963); *Flowers for Hitler* (1964); *Beautiful Losers* (1966); *Parasites of Heaven* (1966); *Selected Poems, 1956-1968* (1968); *The Energy of Slaves* (1972); and *Death of a Lady's Man* (1978).

Works on Cohen include Michael Ondaatje, *Leonard Cohen* (1970); Patricia A. Morley, *The Immoral Moralists: Hugh MacLennan and Leonard Cohen* (1972); Michael Gnarowski, ed., *Leonard Cohen: The Artist and His Critics* (1976); Dennis Lee, *Savage Fields: An Essay in Literature and Cosmology* (1977); and Stephen Scobie, *Leonard Cohen* (1978).

– KEN NORRIS

GEORGE BOWERING

1935-

Born in Penticton, British Columbia, in 1935, George Bow-ering is the author of more than a dozen books and chapbooks of poetry, plus three novels and two collections of short stories. He has won the Governor-General's Award for both poetry (1969) and fiction (1980). Bowering has been involved in the publication of influential magazines such as the poetry newsletter *Tish*, *Imago* and *Open Letter*. He earned B.A. and M.A. degrees at the University of British Columbia. Bowering now lives in Vancouver and teaches American liter-ature at Simon Fraser University.

Having been heavily influenced by Black Mountain poetic theory during the first five years of his public writing life, Bowering produced several volumes of adept open-form lyrics. Poems like "Grandfather" and "Inside the Tulip" il-lustrate the use of the breathline and a fleet movement from one perception to another that Charles Olson insisted upon in his seminal essay "Projective Verse."

In the mid-1960s Bowering became interested in longer poem structures, in the book as a unit of composition, and in the interface between author and personal/social history. In *Autobiology* Bowering penned the line "Consciousness is how it is composed," and his work since that time has served as a record of his personal consciousness and attendant self-consciousness.

Bowering's early serial poem *Baseball* and the poem suite *Rocky Mountain Foot* (for which he won the Governor-General's Award) employed standard forms of poetic exten-sion, utilizing narrative and collage techniques pioneered by the early Moderns. Later works like *Curious* and *Autobiology* are much more interesting and imaginative poems. In *Curious* Bowering offers forty-eight "portraits" of other poets filtered through his own consciousness, while in *Autobiology* he focuses upon moments in his physiological development that altered his consciousness and way of perceiving the world.

Although over the past five years he has tended to concentrate on writing prose fiction, Bowering still publishes the occasional book of occasional verse (*Another Mouth*). Two recent selections of his poetry (*Particular Accidents* and *West Window*) illustrate the diversity and commitment to experimentation that Bowering's work embodies.

In his introduction to the short story anthology *Fiction of Contemporary Canada*, Bowering utilized the analogy of a man watching television while, at the same time, seeing his own reflection in the screen to describe the condition of post-modernism. Bowering's own poetry has reflected a gradual realization of just such a condition; rarely in his recent work are we unaware of the presence of the author and of our own participation in the formulation of the aesthetic experience.

Bowering's works include *Points on the Grid* (1964); *The Silver Wire* (1966); *Rocky Mountain Foot* (1968); *The Gangs of Kosmos* (1969); *Genève* (1971); *In the Flesh* (1974); *A Short Sad Book* (1977); *Burning Water* (1980); *Particular Accidents* (1980); and *West Window* (1982).

Works on Bowering include Ken Norris, "The Poetry of George Bowering," in *Brave New Wave* (1978); Allan Brown, "Beyond the Crenel: A View of George Bowering," *Brick*, No. 6 (1979), pp. 36-39; Robin Blaser, "George Bowering's Plain Song," in *Particular Accidents* (1980); and Ellen Quigley, "*Tish*: Bowering's Infield Position," *Studies in Canadian Literature*, 5 (1980), 23-46.

— KEN NORRIS

JOHN NEWLOVE

1938-

Born in Regina, raised in Verigin and Kamsack, John Newlove graduated from Kamsack Collegiate in 1956. He was a school teacher, a social worker, and a radio announcer before moving to Vancouver, where he met many of the young poets and artists emerging in the early sixties. Two such artists, Robert Reid and Takao Tanabe, published his first collection, *Grave Sirs,* in 1962. Newlove's poems of hitchhiking, history, and heartache quickly caught the critics' and readers' attention; McClelland and Stewart began publishing him in 1968, and later hired him as an editor. During the late seventies he was Writer-in-Residence at a number of institutions, most recently the Public Library in Regina.

At least one critic has suggested that John Newlove is Canada's major poet of the anti-heroic, whose work is full of self-loathing and hatred for the whole human race and its treacherous world. Certainly there are many moments of despair in Newlove's poetry, but equally there are moments of ecstasy, even of joy. And if there is self-hatred, and self-pity alongside envy or hatred of others, there is also a great compassion for those who have been forced to suffer, even if that compassion is articulated in terms of an almost savage wit. Indeed, Newlove can be very funny, sometimes when he is being most serious and profound. Frank Davey says he "has developed one of the most direct and visually precise styles in twentieth-century poetry," in which most of the traditional signs of poetry—simile and metaphor, overt symbolism, rhyme, and heightened language—are missing. Yet Newlove's work *is* poetry, a poetry of great rhythmic subtlety and intensity, in which punning turns of language and careful modulations of tone keep the reader continually off balance. His is a bare-bones poetic, as if he distrusted the riches of language because they tempt one to forms of lying—

bombast, rhetorical flourishes, sentimental overstatement. Art may be the lie that reveals the deeper truth of the imagination, but one must be scrupulously honest in its making if one is not to betray both the language and one's self. Newlove's refusal to give in to the temptations listed above is the major sign of his honesty as an artist. Whether he is writing of the pains of love, the sufferings of natives or early explorers, the anger and ruin of wars, the strange landscapes of dreams, or, sometimes, the momentary delight of wholly being in the world of the senses, he pays close attention to the experience and to the language which will most directly speak it. And even in the rendering of the worst aspects of the human condition, the integrity and energy of the poetry affirm life, humanity, the love the artist bears the world.

Newlove's works include *Grave Sirs* (1962); *Elephants, Mothers and Others* (1963); *Moving in Alone* (1965); *Notebook Pages* (1966); *What They Say* (1967); *Black Night Window* (1968); *The Cave* (1970); *Lies* (1972); and *The Fat Man: Selected Poems* (1977).

Works on Newlove include Margaret Atwood, "How Do I Get Out of Here: The Poetry of John Newlove," *Open Letter*, 2nd ser., No. 4 (1973), 59-70; George Bowering, "Where Does the Truth Lie," *Open Letter*, 2nd ser., No. 4 (1973), 71-74; Jan Bartley, "Something in Which to Believe for Once: The Poetry of John Newlove,"*Open Letter*, 2nd ser., No. 9 (1974), 19-48; Brian Henderson, "Newlove: Poet of Appearance," *Essays on Canadian Writing*, No. 2 (1975), pp. 9-27; and Douglas Barbour, "John Newlove: More Than Just Honest Despair: Some Further Approaches," *Essays on Canadian Writing*, Nos. 18-19 (Summer-Fall 1980), 256-80.

– DOUGLAS BARBOUR

MARGARET ATWOOD

1939-

Margaret Atwood was born in Ottawa on 18 November 1939. She attended high school in Toronto, and received her B.A. from Victoria College, Toronto, in 1961, the year in which she published her first collection of poems, *Double Persephone*. During the late 1950s and early 1960s, she published poems in *The Canadian Forum*, *The Tamarack Review*, *Alphabet*, *The Fiddlehead*, *Delta*, and other periodicals. She received her M.A. from Harvard in 1962. In 1964-65 she lectured in English at the University of British Columbia, and from 1967-68 at Sir George Williams University, Montreal. In 1967 her first full-length book of poems, *The Circle Game*, won a Governor-General's award. With novelist Graeme Gibson she lived for a number of years on their farm near Alliston, Ontario, and they and their daughter now reside in Toronto.

Margaret Atwood works with the traditional substance of lyric poetry: the dramatization of a speaking self in relation to the poet's sense of the world. Her central model is the Romantic reflective lyric, a genre which includes description and imbedded or implicit narrative, but which is focused on thought and feeling. Along with her contemporaries, Margaret Atwood has participated in the modernizing of this model. The traditional reflective lyric, in the simplicities of song or the complexities of the ode, follows some paradigm of sequence; the modern lyric moves toward the fragmentary, at its extreme becoming completely rhapsodic and discontinuous. Atwood is modern in her demotic diction and conversational idiom, in the range of images and fictions in her poetry, in the free verse patterning of her poems, and in eschewing rhyme in favour of assonance; but she keeps to the basic tenet of the reflective lyric, as contrasted with imagistic or modernist collage: the syntax in her later poems may be elliptical, but the connectives of sequence, the copulas of thought—with their implicit trust in the possibility of meaning and their assertion of the presence of the speaking voice—are not relinquished. Her preferred figures of speech—synechdoche, metonymy, simile, irony—suggest an analytical rather than a visual imagination. Her use of revisionary enjambement, oxymoron, and parenthesis suggests a concern with connecting the disparate. Apposition, one of her favourite devices, is also a trope of analogy, a figure of implied equivalence, a mode of connection. Her subjects are central—our involvment with violence, our questionable claims on the world, our mortality, our longing, our consolations; her scope is wide in space and time, reaching back to pre-history and forward to imaginations of catastrophe. She is a threshold poet, looking both ways. Her work is unified by the recurrence of certain images and preoccupations, and it is strong and varied in its occasions and formal arrangements. It accords with Wallace Stevens' description of the supreme fiction: it gives pleasure; it is composed; it changes; and it is human.

Atwood's works include *Double Persephone* (1961); *The Circle Game* (1966); *The Animals in That Country* (1968); *The Journals of Susanna Moodie* (1970); *Procedures for Underground* (1970); *Power Politics* (1971); *You Are Happy* (1974); *Selected Poems* (1976); *Two-Headed Poems* (1978); and *True Stories* (1981).

Works on Atwood include Gloria Onley, "Power Politics in Bluebeard's Castle," *Canadian Literature*, No. 60 (1974), pp. 21-42; Carolyn Allen, "Margaret Atwood: Power of Transformation, Power of Knowledge," *Essays on Canadian Writing* No. 6 (1977), pp. 5-17; Frank Davey, "Atwood's Gorgon Torch," *Studies in Canadian Literature*, 2 (1977), 146-63; Linda Sandler, ed., *Margaret Atwood: A Symposium (The Malahat Review, 1977)*; and Arnold and Cathy Davidson, eds., *The Art of Margaret Atwood: Essays in Criticism* (1981).

– JEAN MALLINSON

bill bissett

1939-

bill bissett presents special difficulties for the anthologist. His paintings and drawings are as integral to his vision as are his spirited performances of sound poetry, which cannot be represented adequately even on recordings, let alone in print. Born in Halifax, bissett moved to Vancouver in the late 1950s—a geographical range appropriate to the expansiveness of his work. Since the middle '60s his blewointmentpress has published about half of his own forty-odd books, as well as many collections of poetry by his contemporaries. His radical styles of life and art have provoked attacks by reviewers, and persecution—extending to prosecution—by police and politicians. But if his unconventional spelling, unabashed vocabulary, and strange concrete poems have offended some, they have fascinated others. "Dirty concrete poet," a phrase in his "pome in praise of all quebec bombers," is not simply a hostile epithet, but also wry self-description.

Concrete poetry stresses the shapes of words or letters (sometimes collaged with pictures), and their unusual deployment on the page. In its density and apparent disarray, "quebec bombers" is an example of "dirty" concrete, a term coined to distinguish such pieces from those with the comparative elegance of bissett's typographical tapestries. Close attention to either kind will reveal that there can be more to such work than meets the eye. As a concrete poet, bissett is often linked with his fellow innovator, bpNichol, but he also has important affinities with certain older Canadian writers. His ironic personal narratives represent a genre which Earle Birney and Al Purdy, among others, have made especially fertile in the past few decades. As well, bissett's prophetic intensity connects him to the Romantic tradition in modern poetry. His work displays an energy and extravagance comparable to Irving Layton's, with the same readiness to yoke

vulgarity and vision, and to go beyond bounds, damn the
consequences. It is no coincidence that bissett, like Layton,
has produced a body of poetry staggering in its mass and
uneven quality, which, at its best, is entertaining and il-
luminating. bissett's roots are in the counterculture of the
1960s, and he still refuses to accept as inevitable our acceler-
ated technological and political damage to nature and the
human community. His early manifesto, "tell me what attackd yu," enacts in its syntax the inclusiveness which has
remained his cardinal poetic principle. His elemental
metaphors (food, breath, light) affirm an eagerness to sustain
all life, including the life of the imagination. He may not even
finally reject technology, despite the "robot stink" of its
excesses, but he would give our inward powers priority —

> for then, in ourselves th best food,
>   we share th bounty
>   on this Iron Horse.

  bissett's works include *we sleep inside each other all* (1966);
awake in th red desert (1968); *Nobody Owns th Earth*
(1971); *th high green hill* (1972); *pomes for yoshi* (1972);
pass th food release th spirit book (1973); *plutonium missing*
(1976); *Selected Poems: Beyond Even Faithful Legends*
(1980); and *northern birds in color* (1981).

  Works on bissett include Frank Davey, *From There to Here*
(1974); Eli Mandel, "Ecological Heroes and Visionary Politics: Contemporary Primitivism in Canadian Writing,"
Rune, No. 2 (1975), pp. 55-67; Len Early, "bill bissett/Poe-
tics, Politics & Vision," *Essays on Canadian Writing*, No. 5
(1976), pp. 4-24; and Jack David, "Visual Poetry in Canada:
Birney, bissett, and bp," *Studies in Canadian Literature*, 2
(1977), 252-66.

                                                    – L. R. EARLY

PATRICK LANE

1939-

Patrick Lane was born at Nelson, British Columbia, but educated at Vernon in the Okanagan Valley to which his family moved in his early childhood. He left school in the early 1950s and never attended a university. Instead he became an unskilled labourer in construction, logging, sawmilling, etc. The example of his brother, the poet Red Lane, led him to begin writing verse in the middle 1960s. His first book appeared in 1966, and since then he has published more than twenty books and broadsheets of poems, and his work has appeared in many literary magazines. He was closely involved in the little poetry-publishing press, Very Stone House, established in 1966 in Vancouver, and in recent years he has been able, through Canada Council grants and spells as writer-in-residence (at Ottawa, Edmonton, Saskatoon) to escape from his early life of poverty and hard work. In 1979 he won the Governor-General's Award for Poetry.

Patrick Lane's poetry has shown over the years a growing mastery of form, from the somewhat undeveloped free verse he was writing in the late 1960s to the technically quite elaborate work he has produced in recent years, which shows a considerable awareness of modernist and post-modernist developments without his noticeably becoming any other poet's disciple.

One is in fact aware of a dual process at work in Lane's development. His poetry is exploratory, in the sense that it is always seeking new ways to define and describe what exists, and a great deal of his early verse is devoted to his own experience of poverty and hard work and of the natural world of British Columbia. There is a hard edge to his view of existence, yet underneath it an angry compassion which emerges with particular strength when he considers the cruelty of man to other creatures and, indeed, the cruelty embedded in the natural world itself. In the human world his compassion reaches to the outcast, to the oppressed, to those whom life has pushed to the edge of despair.

But like all true artists, Lane is impelled not only to explore but also to invent, and in recent years his inclination has been towards technical experiment and also towards that tendency to consider history as the vehicle of myth which is found in so many contemporary Canadian writers. Lane had always had a special eye for place, and even in his early poems he showed an extraordinary ability to evoke the landscape of British Columbia with a kind of anatomical sharpness that probed right into its rocky bones. Lately he has developed an ear for history, and some of his recent poems develop in a very interesting way the theme of the relativity of pasts; the suggestion that the unrecorded history of peoples without writing may be as important as those of elaborately literate peoples. This is of course a development of his abiding concern for the forgotten people of the world. A preoccupation with myth, which is history for the non-literate, is always likely to lead into an interest in fantasy, and one of the most striking features of Lane's poems is the way in which he has moved on from sharply represented actuality of so many of his earlier pieces into a world of sometimes bizarre invention.

Lane's works include *Letters from the Savage Mind* (1966); *Separations* (1969); *Mountain Oysters* (1971); *Beware the Months of Fire* (1974); *Unborn Things* (1975); *Albino Pheasants* (1977); *Poems New and Selected* (1978); *The Measure* (1980); and *Old Mother* (1982).

Works on Lane include Marilyn Bowering, "Pine Boughs and Apple Trees: The Poetry of Patrick Lane," *The Malahat Review*, No. 45 (1978); and Jean Mallinson, "A Reading of Pat Lane," *Brick*, No. 7 (1979), pp. 5-8.

— GEORGE WOODCOCK

DENNIS LEE

1939-

Dennis Lee was born and raised in Toronto, attending the University of Toronto Schools and Victoria College in the University of Toronto, where he received his honours B.A. in English literature in 1962. After a year in England he returned to the University of Toronto to earn his M.A. and to teach at Victoria College for four years. Then, driven by an awareness of what he saw as the university's failure to emancipate the mind and imagination and spirit, he transferred as resource person to the Rochdale cooperative and joined with Howard Adelman, another cooperative supporter, to edit a collection of essays critical of establishment education. *The University Game* (1968) was published by House of Anansi Press, which Dave Godfrey and he had founded the previous year; and when Rochdale failed, Lee gave his attention to Anansi as chief editor. In the next six years Anansi published the first novels of a number of talented newcomers: Ray Smith, Matt Cohen, Graeme Gibson. Since then, although still a publisher's consultant, Lee has been a full-time poet and critic.

As a poet, Dennis Lee's subject has been his anguish at the failure of his society to provide authentic values by which to live. His thought has been greatly influenced by two theologians, Martin Heidegger and George Grant. From Heidegger, Lee learned that man could only fully possess himself and be at home in nature when he recognized the sacredness of all being. Individual human beings, surrounded by the emptiness of space and riddled with the emptiness of time — continual change moving relentlessly towards disintegration — live with the temptation to retreat into postures of defiant despair. Such postures become the only available responses within a liberal ideology that separates consciousness from nature, elevates individual consciousness as the source of all meaning and value, and debases nature to an alien external that might be dominated by technology. From Grant, Lee learned that Canada, by existing, presumes an alternative to the liberal values which, arising in Renaissance Europe, have taken their most progressive and dominant forms in the United States. To illuminate man's plight of diminished consciousness while hinting at absent fuller possibilities, Lee developed his free verse approximations of traditional verse forms. His early attempts with sonnets were not very successful since the sonnet is a Renaissance form and therefore part of the affliction. Lee has been more successful with the elegy and ode, sonorous public verse forms that reach back to classical Greece.

Lee's works include *Kingdom of Absence* (1967); *Civil Elegies* (1968; revised, and with two additional elegies, 1972); and *The Gods* (1979). In addition he has written a number of works for children, including *Alligator Pie* (1974), *Nicholas Knock* (1974), and *Garbage Delight* (1977); and a few critical pieces, the most important being "Cadence, Country, Silence" in *Liberté* (1972) and *Savage Fields: An Essay in Literature and Cosmology* (1977).

Works on Dennis Lee include Marilyn Baxter, "I Patched My Coat with Darkness," *Acta Victoriana*, 92, No. 4 (1968), 18-24; Frank Davey, "Dennis Lee," in *From There to Here* (1974); D. G. Jones, "In Search of Canada: Dennis Lee's Ironic Vision," *ARC* (Carleton University) 1 (1978), 23-28; and *Descant*, (1982).

– TOM MIDDLEBRO'

GWENDOLYN MACEWEN

1941-

Born in Toronto, Gwendolyn MacEwen had her first poem published when she was fifteen. Three years later she left school to devote herself to a literary career. This was propitious because at that time Canadian literature was embarking on a path of new popularity and growth. Her talent made her one of the new and bright lights in that development. Mac-Ewen's first book was published in 1961, and since then she has published seven more books of poems, two novels, a collection of stories, a play, and written verse dramas for radio as well as the libretto for a jazz cantata. *The Shadow-Maker* (1969) won the Governor-General's Award for poetry. MacEwen has also won a CBC New Writing contest (1965), the Borestone Mountain Poetry Award, and been awarded several Canada Council grants. She is a world-traveller with a deep interest in the development, religion, and literature of ancient Egypt and Greece.

In her poems MacEwen creates a world that is at once beautiful and harsh, magical and familiar, painful and ecstatic. Her interest in the cultures of ancient civilizations has resulted in her becoming one of the few Canadian poets whose work benefits from an applied knowledge of Classical mythologies. She can thus be placed in the mythological tradition of W.B. Yeats and Robert Graves. But her interest is directed not only to the traditional components of mythic poetry—the journey, gods and goddesses, the counterpoint of creation and destruction, incantatory rhetoric, the Muse. It is also directed toward perceiving and creating mythic experiences in the everyday, contemporary world. Some conservative critics consider such attempts to be inherently false, a kind of posturing. But in fact MacEwen's sensibility allows for the existence of the old gods and the creation of new ones, be they felt in the air of a room or invented in attempts to give meaning to a particularly intense or puzzling experience. In this context, it is possible that "all worlds, all times, all loves are one." Such convictions about art and culture both set MacEwen apart from the mainstream of contemporary Canadian poetry and allow her to seek (and sometimes see) a universal vision in which all the various manifestations and permutations of life can be suddenly integrated and understood.

MacEwen's works include *The Rising Fire* (1963); *Julian the Magician* (1963); *A Breakfast for Barbarians* (1966); *The*

Shadow-Maker (1969); *King of Egypt, King of Dreams* (1971); *Noman* (1972); *Mermaids and Ikons* (1977); *The Trojan Women* (1979); *The T. E. Lawrence Poems* (1982); and *Earthlight: The Selected Poetry of Gwendolyn MacEwen 1963-1982* (1982).

Works on MacEwen include Margaret Atwood, "Mac-Ewen's Muse," *Canadian Literature*, No. 45 (1970), pp. 24-32; and Ellen D. Warwick, "To Seek a Single Symmetry," *Canadian Literature*, No. 71 (1976), pp. 21-34.

– ROBERT BILLINGS

DAPHNE MARLATT

1942-

Daphne Marlatt was born in Melbourne, Australia, and grew up in Penang, Malaysia, until her family immigrated to Canada in 1951. At the University of British Columbia in the early sixties, she studied with Warren Tallman and Robert Creeley and attended the Poetry Conference in the summer of 1963. She did post-graduate work at Indiana University and lived for a time in Wisconsin, before returning to Vancouver (the imaginative "ground" of her vision) with her son, Kit, where she has since lived. She has taught at Capilano College, helped edit *The Capilano Review*, co-edited *periodics*, been an oral-historian for the B.C. Provincial Archives, and published ten books of her own writing.

"All my poetics are, is connections," says Daphne Marlatt in an interview with George Bowering, and that succinctly states how her poetry works. Later, she adds, "the truth is like a palimpsest—all the layers *at once*, all the levels at once," and what some readers might at first find "difficult" in her work are her precise attempts to give us "all the layers *at once*" of an experience—the perception of *it all*. Marlatt has been called a "phenomenological" writer because she insists both on encountering the world out there as fully as possible

316

and on minutely and painstakingly examining the processes of perception by which her consciousness articulates each encounter. Thus what we discover in the act of reading her poem is *her* act of discovering what she *had* (in front of her, to reach out and touch) *to say.* Slowly Marlatt accumulates perceptions and the articulations of them. She does not simply *tell us about* situations, events, feelings; rather she pulls us into a series of complexly lived processes which can be experienced poetically only in a cumulative flow of words and phrases marking the movements of her own perceptions as they occur. Her own perceptions include not just what she sees or hears, but what she feels through all her senses, what she reads, whatever touches her responsive being as she encounters a failing fishing town, a lover, a night sky and the knowledge of riots, or whatever else in her world her consciousness might light upon: to perceive it, whole. Her poetics insist on openness both to the phenomena of perception and emotion and to the self-governing structures of language as a medium of (meditative) exploration. Although the "meaning" of her densely woven nets of "inscape" is simply their being in us, a political commitment to the need for true perception before any action can be socially useful is implicit.

Marlatt's works include *Frames of a Story* (1968); *leaf leaf/s* (1968); *Rings* (1971); *Vancouver Poems* (1972); *Steveston* (1974); *Our Lives* (1975; 1980); *The Story, She Said* (1977); *Zócalo* (1977); *What Matters: Writing 1968-70* (1980); and *Net Work: Selected Writing* (1980).

Works on Marlatt include Frank Davey, "Daphne Marlatt," *From There to Here* (1974); Robert Lecker, "Daphne Marlatt's Poetry," *Canadian Literature,* No. 76 (1978), pp. 56-67; Jack Silver, "Moving into Winter: A Study of Daphne Marlatt's *Our Lives,*" *Open Letter,* 3rd. ser., No. 8 (1978), 89-103; Douglas Barbour, "The Phenomenological I: Daphne Marlatt's *Steveston,*" *Figures in a Ground: Canadian Essays on Modern Literature Collected in Honor of Sheila Watson,* ed. Diane Bessai and David Jackel (1978); and George Bowering, "Given This Body: an interview with Daphne Marlatt," *Open Letter,* 4th ser., No. 3 (1979), 32-88.

– DOUGLAS BARBOUR

MICHAEL ONDAATJE

1943-

Michael Ondaatje was born in Ceylon, studied in England, and since 1962 has been in Canada, where he is now a citizen. He currently teaches English at Glendon College, York University. He divides the year between Toronto and a farm north of Kingston, Ontario. Ondaatje's third book of poetry, *The Collected Works of Billy the Kid* (1970), won the Governor-General's Award; and *Coming Through Slaughter* (1976) was co-winner of the *Books in Canada* First Novel Award. Stage productions of both works have been seen in Canada and, in the case of *Billy*, in the U.S. Ondaatje's films include *Sons of Captain Poetry*, on bpNichol, and *Clinton Special*, on Theatre Passe Muraille's *The Farm Show*.

Ondaatje's poetry explores fundamentals of the male and female heart, the relation of man to animal and to machine, and the process of creation. Like much contemporary art, Ondaatje's retrieves and reshapes information from history, myth, and legend, including the pop culture dominating sensibilities formed in the 1950s and '60s. From this wide subject span, he creates both extreme situations and domestic harmonies. The longer works expose the reader to intense pain, fear, and violence located in grotesques—transformed figures seeking a voice and a metaphor, caught between normalcy and insanity, killer and gentleman, human and savage. Dissecting them, Ondaatje's technical control rivals that of his "sane assassin," Pat Garrett. Ondaatje's is a taut line, his acute sense of detail sharpening the reader's focus on living reality.

We begin with a familiar subject and it explores us. Like the blind poet-lover not knowing what he loves until he writes it out ("The gate in his head'") and the spider thinking a path and then travelling it ("Spider Blues"), Ondaatje creates and discovers at the same time. *Catch, freeze, immobilize, collect,* and *photograph* suggest recording devices for realities masked in whiteness, night,

318

and ambiguity. The nature of reality, even in the domestic world, is so complex that it must be isolated from the flux of time and reconstituted at leisure. Paradoxically, for Ondaaje it is reality itself which is our *terra incognita;* and his metaphors of globe, town, path, road, flight, arc, and landscape invoke process and journey as models of creation. Like the 20th-century physicist, Ondaatje demonstrates that the very instruments, models, and media of perception alter the thing observed. And so the observer must be devious and ambidextrous in conveying "the sense of shift" in the living reality. Ondaatje's ambiguities, refracted vision, and tension between heated subject and cool observer aim to catch the thing without, spider-like, destroying it:

> And that is all this writing should be then.
> The beautiful formed things caught at the wrong moment
> so they are shapeless, awkward
> moving to the clear.

Ondaatje's works include *The Dainty Monsters* (1967); *The Man with Seven Toes* (1969); *Leonard Cohen* (1969); *The Collected Works of Billy the Kid* (1970); *Rat Jelly* (1973); *Coming Through Slaughter* (1976); and *There's A Trick with a Knife I'm Learning to Do* (1979).

Works on Ondaatje include Sheila Watson, "Michael Ondaatje: The Mechanization of Death," *White Pelican,* No. 2 (1972), pp. 56-64; Anne Blott, "Stories to Finish: *The Collected Works of Billy the Kid,*" *Studies in Canadian Literature* 2 (1977), 188-202; Stephen Scobie, "His Legend a Jungle Sleep: Michael Ondaatje and Henri Rousseau," *Canadian Literature,* No. 76 (1978), pp. 6-21; and Sam Solecki, "Nets and Chaos: The Poetry of Michael Ondaatje," *Brave New Wave* (1978).

— ANNE BLOTT

bpNICHOL

1944-

bpNichol was born in Vancouver in 1944, and attended the
University of British Columbia. Since 1964, he has lived in
Toronto, where he works with the therapeutic community,
Therafields. As early as 1963, he began to be interested in the
international movement known as "concrete poetry," and he
has published steadily and productively since 1965. He won
the Governor-General's Award for Poetry in 1970. Nichol
forms part of the experimental sound-poetry group, The Four
Horsemen, which has performed together since 1970. He and
his wife Ellie have one daughter, Sarah, born in 1981.

bpNichol's favourite description of himself is as an "apprentice to language." This phrase suggests that his work is to
be regarded as exploratory. It also stresses the primacy of
language in Nichol's world-view; he refers often to the myth
of the god Palongowhoya, who set the vibratory axis of the
world in motion by the rhythms of his own breath and speech.

Diversity of form, and continual exploration of the varying
modes of language, thus become constants in Nichol's work.
He has written traditional, open form, free verse poetry;
concise lyrics; and long, sprawling, book-length poems. He
has written and designed visual poems, which depend for their
effect on the collaboration of a typographer or a visual artist.
He has drawn comic strips and poems based on comic strips.
He has written poems in which words are replaced by individual letters. He has designed whole new alphabets. He has
created poems out of Polaroid photographs. He has written
"novels" the length of short stories. He has written prose
narrative in stream-of-consciousness style, in the convoluted
repetitive style derived from Gertrude Stein, in the forms of
the Western and the detective story, and as a collage of letters,
parodies, journals, etc. He has written theoretical essays and
manifestos. He has written "translations," in a wide variety
of experimental forms, from other languages and from Eng-

lish into English, as "homolinguistic" translation. He has created sound poems, some of which use tape technology, most of which do not. In all these fields he has worked both solo and in collaboration. There is scarcely a conceivable form of literary activity which bpNichol has not touched, tried, and transformed.

But the diversity of this research will never be fully appreciated unless its consistency is also appreciated, and that consistency is to be found in the humanist base of all Nichol's writing. The task of the poet, he wrote in 1967, consists of "finding as many exits as possible from the self (language / communication exits) in order to form as many entrances as possible for the other. the other is the loved one and the other the key . . . . traditional poetry is only one of the means by which to reach out and touch the other. The other is emerging as the necessary prerequisite for dialogues with the self that clarify the soul & heart and deepen the ability to love." Whether that "other" is defined as lover or language, this statement still stands as the essence of Nichol's poetic.

bpNichol's published works include *Journeying & the returns* (1967); *Two Novels* (1969); *Still Water* (1970); *ABC: the aleph beth book* (1971); *The Martyrology* (Books 1 and 2, 1972; Books 3 and 4, 1976); *Love: a Book of Remembrances* (1974); *Craft Dinner* (1978); *Journal* (1978); *Translating Translating Apollinaire* (1979); *As Elected: Selected Writing 1962-1979* (1980); and *extreme positions* (1981).

Interviews with bpNichol include Caroline Bayard and Jack David in *Out-Posts/Avant-Postes* (1978); and Ken Norris, "Interview with bp Nichol: Feb. 13, 1978," *Essays on Canadian Writing*, No. 12 (1978), pp. 243-50. Essays on Nichol include Jack David, "Writing Writing: bpNichol at 30," *Essays on Canadian Writing*, No. 1 (1974), pp. 37-48; Roderick W. Harvey, "bpNichol: The Repositioning of Language," *Essays on Canadian Writing*, No. 4 (1976), pp. 19-33; and Stephen Scobie, "The Words You Trust to Take You Thru: An Introduction to bpNichol's The Martyrology," *Precisely: One* (1977). A major study of Nichol's work is included in Brian Henderson, *Radical Poetics* (Diss. York 1982).

– STEPHEN SCOBIE